SOCIAL-EMOTIONAL LEARNING in the ENGLISH LANGUAGE CLASSROOM

Fostering Growth, Self-Care, and Independence

Luis Javier Pentón Herrera
and Gilda Martinez-Alba

www.tesol.org/bookstore

TESOL International Association
1925 Ballenger Avenue
Alexandria, VA 22314 USA
www.tesol.org

Group Director, Content and Learning: Myrna Jacobs
Copy Editor: Tomiko Breland
Production Editor: Tomiko Breland
Manuscript Reviewers: Elsa Anderson, Jessica Burchett, Rabia Hos,
    Patricia Reynolds, Stefani Roth
Cover Design: Citrine Sky Design
Design and Layout: Capitol Communications, LLC

Recommended citation:
Pentón Herrera, L. J., & Martínez-Alba, G. (2021). *Social-emotional learning
in the English language classroom: Fostering growth, self-care, and independence.*
TESOL International Association.

ISBN 978-1-953745-02-6
ISBN (ebook) 978-1-953745-03-3
Library of Congress Control Number 2021940270

Table of Contents

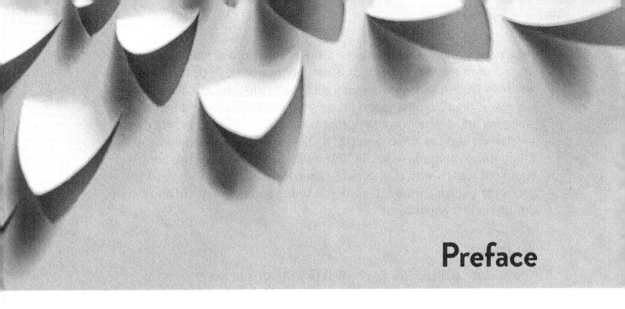

Preface

The practice of social-emotional learning (SEL) has been growing in the United States and around the world for some years. Presently, many public and private educational systems, community organizations, and higher education institutions embrace SEL practices in various forms, such as wellness conversations, mindfulness interventions, trauma-informed instruction, restorative circles, and yoga. The incorporation of SEL practices is undoubtedly experiencing a *momentum*, as Collaborative for Academic, Social, and Emotional Learning (CASEL; 2013) calls it, and its popularity is expected to become increasingly necessary in our schools, learning spaces, and society.

The recent global events that we all are experiencing, such as global pandemics, natural disasters, religious persecutions, forced migrations, social and political unrest, and violence, are reminding us of our interconnectedness as global citizens. At the same time, society and employers are now, more than ever, in desperate need of individuals who are emotionally intelligent (Harvard Business Review, 2015). Employers are looking for individuals who

- have the capacity to recognize and regulate their own emotions;
- are capable of empathizing with others;
- have the ability to establish and maintain healthy, rewarding relationships with diverse people; and
- are able to make constructive and respectful choices and decisions (Committee for Children, 2016a, 2016b).

Through SEL, educational institutions are able to equip students and adults with the necessary technical, academic, and social-emotional skills they need to succeed in their lives after school.

This book originates from our increased awareness of the critical need to equip our English learners (ELs) "with essential skills to succeed as *students* in schools, as *professionals* in their future, and as *human beings* in life" (Pentón Herrera, 2020, p. 2). More specifically, we hope this resource will help English language teaching (ELT) professionals learn about and use SEL in their learning spaces. At present, this book is one of limited emerging SEL resources available that is tailored to the teachers of English to speakers of other languages (TESOL) field and that is contributing to filling the existing gap of SEL in TESOL education. We hope this book will equip our readers with the necessary knowledge and skills they need to feel confident implementing SEL in their learning spaces to support and benefit our EL student population.

Audience

The primary audience for this book is practitioners in the ELT field at large. More specifically, teachers in K–12 and adult education, and teacher educators in pre- and in-service TESOL teacher preparation programs in the United States and around the world.

Purpose and Overview

The purpose of this book is to serve as a guide that ELT practitioners at all levels can use to incorporate SEL in their classrooms. Teachers often feel unprepared to incorporate or address SEL in their classrooms and do not know the *how-to* of SEL (Brackett, 2019). As authors, our vision is that this book will serve as a practical, concise, and easy-to-follow reference that English language teachers in K–12 and adult education and TESOL teacher educators can use in their classrooms.

Annotated Table of Contents

This book presents SEL principles and practices in two parts and six chapters:

Part I: Preparing for Social-Emotional Learning

- **Chapter 1. Introducing Social-Emotional Learning in English Language Teaching** introduces SEL, discusses key SEL core competencies, makes a case for SEL in ELT, and discusses considerations teachers should have when incorporating SEL into their learning spaces. It also provides an overview of the content readers will find in the rest of the book.

- **Chapter 2. Social-Emotional Learning in Teacher Preparation Programs** proposes ideas of how TESOL teacher educators can incorporate SEL into their pre- or in-service teacher education programs. It also outlines nine common SEL frameworks and shares activities that teacher educators can use to integrate SEL in their courses.

- **Chapter 3. Teacher Self-Care and Well-Being** proposes teacher self-care and well-being as the foundation for the effective incorporation of SEL. It provides an overview of teacher self-care, shares practical applications, and ends with additional materials that teachers can use right away to incorporate self-care into their daily practices.

Part II. Practical Applications of Social-Emotional Learning

- **Chapter 4. Mindfulness** defines and shares an overview of mindfulness attitudes and shows how mindfulness can be integrated into English language classrooms through three practical lessons.

- **Chapter 5. Peace Education** shows how peace education can be integrated into English language classrooms. It provides an overview of peace education, shares three lessons of practical applications, and ends with additional materials teachers can use in their classrooms.

- **Chapter 6. Restorative Practices** provides an overview of restoration and restorative practices and explains how they can be integrated into English language classrooms through three practical lessons.

A necessary clarification that we would like to add for our readers about Chapters 4 through 6 is that the information we share about these three SEL practices (i.e., mindfulness, peace education, and restorative practices) can be modified to meet your specific learning context's needs and your ELs' language levels. SEL is a process, not a program. This means that its practices and frameworks can be modified to fit into any learning context, for any age group, and for any language proficiency. SEL has no limitations; practitioners can modify SEL practices to fit their learning realities, students' necessities, and subjects taught.

> **" SOCIAL-EMOTIONAL LEARNING IS A PROCESS, NOT A PROGRAM. "**

ACKNOWLEDGMENTS

We are grateful to every single individual who supported us in the making of this book. In particular, we would like to extend our deepest gratitude to each of the teachers featured in this book (in order of appearance): Rochelle Knox, Stephanie Ledger, Nikia Darden, Mamiko Nakata, Ethan Trinh, Tina Ruiz, Kristen Viig, Brian Boyd, May F. Chung, Manuel De Jesús Gómez Portillo, Paulina Kurevija, Christel Young, Robin L. McNair, and Michelle Ivette Marrero Colón.

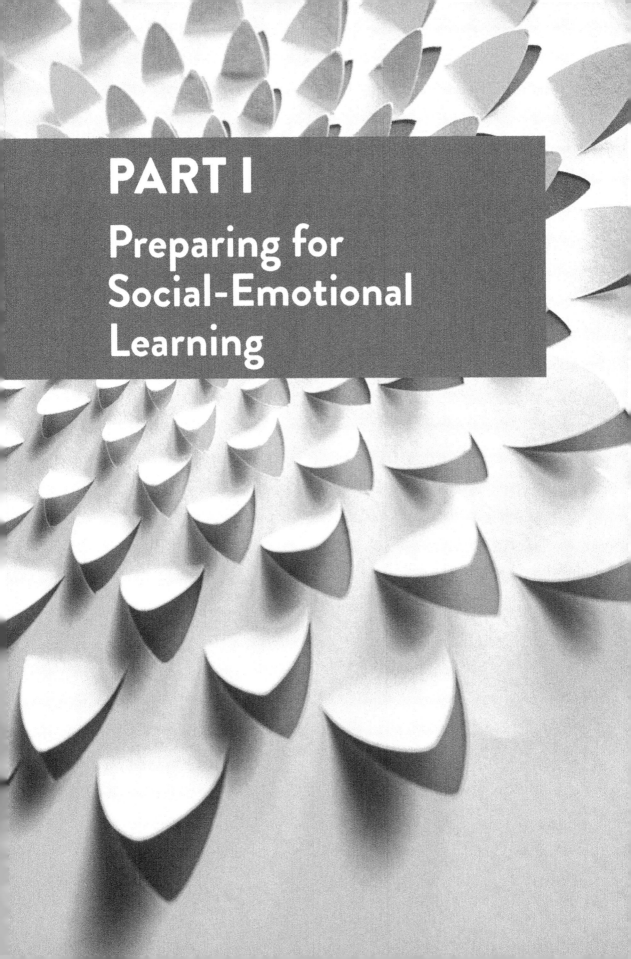

PART I
Preparing for Social-Emotional Learning

CHAPTER 1

Introducing Social-Emotional Learning in English Language Teaching

"The children who need love the most will always ask for it in the most unloving ways."
(Barkley, 2020, p. 5)

MARIELA'S STORY

Mariela[1] is an 18-year-old English learner (EL) who recently arrived in the United States. Upon arrival, Mariela was placed in 9th grade because of her English proficiency level and also because she had some gaps in formal schooling. Mariela's mother and father left their native country of El Salvador when Mariela was 7 years of age; when she arrived in the United States, she reunited with them after being separated for 11 years. Because Mariela grew up primarily with her grandfather in El Salvador and only spoke to her parents occasionally, she did not have the opportunity to establish strong bonds of communication with them. When she arrived in the United States, Mariela and her parents began having disagreements, which were exacerbated by the lack of communication.

In school, Mariela was having a difficult time establishing supportive human connections with her peers. She often made jokes in the classroom, laughed out loud, and attracted her classmates' attention during instruction. Her English as a second language (ESL) teacher firmly asked her many times to stop talking and distracting her classmates, but Mariela would just laugh out loud in response. Because Mariela's behavior was not improving, the ESL teacher called Mariela's parents one day as a final measure. In hopes of receiving parental support, the teacher shared with Mariela's parents the situation he was having in their classroom. While talking to Mariela's parents on the phone, Mariela's

---

[1] All names used in the stories told throughout this book are pseudonyms.

father requested, "*Maestro, por favor, mande a Mariela a un centro de detención para jóvenes, nosotros no sabemos qué hacer con ella tampoco* [Teacher, please, send Mariela to a juvenile detention center, we do not know what to do with her either]." The ESL teacher, shocked, explained to the parents that this was not something he could do, and the conversation ended at that juncture. Mariela's misbehavior continued for a couple of weeks following that phone call, and, after being escorted out of the classroom a few times, Mariela stopped attending school.

This vignette was a real-life story that happened to me, Luis, during my first year as a high school ESL teacher. As a novice educator, I had been trained to focus on my students' academic progress and English language learning. At the same time, I had been taught that classroom management was about control and discipline, not about building personal relationships with students. These statements may sound familiar for some of our readers because these practices continue to be the case at many traditional schools in the United States and around the world today.

Often, the methods adopted at educational institutions are designed in such a way that teachers are forced to identify children as problems instead of recognizing that children are students *with* problems (Ladson-Billings, 2009; Milner et al., 2019). As we write these sentences, we recall comments shared by coworkers in the teacher lounges and around the school: *Guanjie is a problem student*, or *Juanita is trouble!* When we perceive students this way, we automatically dehumanize them; furthermore, we fail to realize that, as young people *with* struggles, our students need our help.

While reflecting on my first year as a novice ESL teacher, I (Luis) have come to terms with the reality that I failed Mariela. Back then, I did not know the concept of educating the *whole child*; instead, I focused on teaching English and literacy because I associated them with a successful life in the United States. However, although English and literacy are undoubtedly crucial for ELs, they only constitute half of the skills my students will need to thrive and become successful members of their new society. Looking back, I realize I was placing too much importance on my students' academic and language development. I failed to recognize Mariela as a student, a young person, with personal conflicts and problems. Perhaps, if I had created a space where Mariela and my other students had the opportunity to develop an awareness of their emotions and how their actions affected those around them, our class would have become a learning community, and Mariela would have made strong bonds with other classmates and me. Perhaps, if I would have incorporated activities where my students had the opportunity to develop literacy, language, and social-emotional skills simultaneously, Mariela would have stayed in school.

Witnessing my students' social-emotional struggles throughout the years made me realize that academics were only one part of the equation for their success. In many instances, my students were not able to fully participate or were not mentally present in our learning spaces because of social-emotional conflicts they were battling alone. I began to make shifts in my teaching practices. I started to incorporate activities in our daily routines where we could explore essential topics, such as feelings (see Pentón Herrera, 2019), emotions (see Pentón Herrera, 2020), and human relationships (see Pentón Herrera & McNair, 2021), all while learning language and literacy. This shift in my pedagogy and teaching made a profound change in my students, our teacher-student relationships, and their overall success. Through the incorporation of more humane teaching practices,[2] I began to acknowledge that social-emotional well-being is just as important as academic development because both contribute to students' well-rounded education.

Background: From Exclusion to Inclusion

The traditional school curriculum—focused on reproduction of content, memorization, teacher-led instruction, and punishment—is affecting our students. This statement is certainly true for vulnerable and minority student populations (Milner et al., 2019; Winn et al., 2019) who continue to have fewer opportunities for success in school and life. At the same time, the traditional school curriculum ignores essential factors (e.g., social, economic, racial, cultural, religious, emotional, and psychological), which often contribute to inequity in learning spaces as well as in society as a whole. As teachers, many times we feel like we are "teaching 21st-century students in 20th-century buildings with a 19th-century educational design" (Eitner, 2018, slide 1). Thankfully, the field of education

---

[2] In this book, we use the term *humane teaching practices* to express our focus on teaching the student while acknowledging their humanity, backgrounds, and life experiences instead of teaching at the student with the purpose of meeting testing and achievement benchmarks.

is experiencing a transformative paradigm shift in recent years where teachers, administrators, teacher educators, and scholars are realizing that traditional teaching practices do not work.

In the 21st century, we have begun to embrace the adoption of more humane teaching practices emphasizing equity, restoration, social justice, inclusion, differentiation, and social-emotional support (Cardimona, 2018; Coady et al., 2016; Hastings & Jacob, 2016; Ladson-Billings, 1995; Moore, 2016; Paris, 2012; Pentón Herrera, 2020, 2021; Pentón Herrera & McNair, 2021; Tantillo Philibert, 2018). These transformative, humane practices enlighten our understanding that schools need to be institutions responsible for ensuring that all learners receive the equitable support to learn and progress in said school. Also, as advocates and moral change agents, teachers are increasingly tasked with ensuring students are gaining the vital skills they will need to succeed in their lives after graduation. This is certainly true for English educators, who "stand at the very heart of the most crucial educational, cultural, and political issues of our time" (Gee, 1989, p. 60). English language teachers are ELs' gatekeepers, ensuring their academic success and their social-emotional well-being. One way to guarantee that ELs develop academic, social, and emotional skills simultaneously is through the integration of social-emotional learning (SEL) opportunities in our learning spaces.

What Is Social-Emotional Learning?

Multiple definitions and understandings of SEL currently exist in the literature. However, in this book, we use Osher et al.'s (2016) definition, in which SEL is the processes "by which children and adults acquire and apply competencies to recognize and manage emotions, set and achieve positive goals, appreciate the perspectives of others, establish and maintain supportive relationships, make responsible decisions, and handle personal and interpersonal situations constructively" (p. 645). Though the acronym "SEL" was developed in 1994 (CASEL, 2020b), SEL-related scholarship and practices can be traced back to the early 1900s (Osher et al., 2016). SEL's fundamental goals are to promote positive, supportive, engaging, and participatory learning environments that prepare learners to succeed in school and their lives as future members of society and the world. SEL's five core competencies "support the message that educating children in social, behavioral, and emotional skills is important to achieve and be successful in school, their societies, and in life" (Pentón Herrera, 2020, p. 3). As you go through the activities in this book, you will see how they correlate to the following five SEL Core Competencies.

SEL Core Competencies

- **Self-awareness:** The ability to recognize one's own emotions and values, to accurately assess weaknesses and strengths, and to possess a well-grounded sense of self-efficacy and optimism

- **Self-management:** The ability to regulate emotions, thoughts, and behaviors in diverse situations, including the ability to manage stress, control impulses, and set and achieve goals
- **Social awareness:** The ability to adopt the perspective of those with different backgrounds, understand social and cultural norms, and recognize available resources and supports
- **Relationship skills:** The ability to establish positive relationships with different kinds of people, communicating clearly, listening actively, cooperating, resisting inappropriate peer pressure, negotiating conflict, and seeking help when necessary
- **Responsible decision-making:** The capacity to make choices based on realistic evaluations of consequences, well-being, ethics, safety, and social norms (CASEL, 2020a; Osher et al., 2016)

A necessary clarification is that, although different frameworks exist, SEL is an approach, not a program (Tantillo Philibert, 2018). This means that SEL practices are flexible and must be tailored to each student's academic, linguistic, physical, emotional, and mental needs. SEL cannot be one-size-fits-all. For this reason, SEL practices are diverse, and the term serves as an umbrella, embracing mindfulness interventions, yoga, bibliotherapy, restorative practices, peace education, trauma-informed practices, emotional intelligence-focused instruction, team-building and community-building activities, as well as other in-school and out-of-school initiatives focusing on student wellness and well-being. Through the incorporation of SEL, students develop their emotional intelligence (an individual's ability to know and manage their emotions, motivate themselves, recognize others' emotions, and handle relationships; Goleman, 2005) and self-regulation and become more aware of their emotions and reactions to them—all of which are tools and skills individuals need to succeed in life (Brackett, 2019; Goleman, 2005; Srinivasan, 2019; Tantillo Philibert, 2018).

Why SEL in English Language Teaching?

ELs are a highly diverse population of students from all over the world, with rich, unique experiences academically, socially, and emotionally. Within the EL population, we can find gifted students; learners with adequate, limited, or interrupted formal education; and learners with special learning needs or with prior schooling that does not align with Western formal education practices. In addition to having diverse academic backgrounds, ELs also have various social-emotional experiences and needs through no fault of their own. For example, in our ESL classroom, we might have students who come from wealthy families in their native countries, Indigenous children escaping structural discrimination and persecution (see Pentón Herrera, 2018), unaccompanied minors, children coming from refugee camps and war-torn countries, as well as resilient young people who are survivors of "intergenerational trauma" (Urrieta, 2019, p. 1).

The diversity of the EL student population is not new for English language practitioners. In fact, our increasing understanding of the rich diversity of this population is why English language educators have become aware that advocacy (Linville, 2016; Staehr Fenner, 2014) is a necessary component of our pedagogy. At the same time, we often become our school buildings' point of contact for translation services, instructional support, differentiation, parent communication, or any other EL-related matter. In many ways, English language educators engage in exemplary teaching principles to ensure ELs have opportunities to achieve academic development and success in our school. Though providing equitable access to learning is vital, it is only half of the skills our ELs need to be successful in school and later in their lives as adults. As young people transitioning into a new country, learning a new language, reuniting and/or separating from family members, and dealing with social-emotional struggles from life experiences as well as from age-appropriate development, our ELs need our help understanding, learning how to manage, and expressing their emotions in a healthy manner.

Many times, ELs have to learn English while also navigating the unwritten social-emotional practices of their new host country. Adopting SEL practices provides a framework for attending to our students' social-emotional needs while transforming English language classrooms into safe and caring learning environments. In addition, the incorporation of SEL in the English language classroom constitutes part of our responsibilities as their advocates, educators, and professionals following exemplary teaching principles (Short et al., 2018). More important, SEL practices give all of our ELs the opportunity to learn the necessary skills they will need to succeed in their future, such as adopting a growth mindset, prioritizing self-care, engaging in emotional management and self-regulation, building and maintaining healthy relationships, and becoming contributing members of their society. In addition to teaching our students English and literacy, we must also understand the responsibility we have to equip our learners with the social-emotional skills they will need to flourish in their new environments.

Considerations for SEL in Action

Similar to any other academic learning experiences, SEL requires planning for successful implementation. In this section, we offer six considerations English language educators should contemplate prior to or while incorporating SEL into their classrooms. As you read these considerations, keep an open mind and make connections to your teaching reality.

1. SEL Is Transformative

When educators choose to integrate SEL in their classrooms, they must make the conscious decision to transform their pedagogy. SEL, as a daily practice, requires guidance and commitment from everyone involved. This means that educators must understand that introducing SEL into their learning spaces requires a transformation of teacher pedagogy, mindset, and thinking.

In practical terms, this transformation translates to disrupting traditional power structures and routines in the learning space. For example, instead of using the term *classroom management* to describe the process where instruction time is not compromised by disruptive behavior, SEL practitioners may choose to think of this process as *classroom coexistence*. From this transformative SEL lens, teachers and students recognize that the classroom does not belong to one person—traditionally, to the teacher. Instead, the classroom transforms into a place where everyone is responsible for maintaining order, rather than being a one-sided, controlled environment. Other practical examples of how SEL practices transform our pedagogy are (1) praising in public, mentoring in private; (2) recognizing that respectful relationships among teacher-student and student-student are vital; and (3) acknowledging that learning begins with listening to others with an open heart and respect—to name a few.

THINK BOX

SEL practitioners often engage in self-reflection to understand their own emotions, biases, and pedagogy. As role models, teachers embracing SEL use the information they learn through self-reflection to guide their present and future growth. Take a moment to reflect on your current practices. Jot down up to five beliefs, practices, and/or routines you would like to transform as you begin to include SEL in your learning space. Keep reading to learn more information about this topic. Then, return to your responses and reflect on how you can improve them.

2. Emotions and Language Matter

In SEL-informed classrooms, teachers and students understand that emotions have the power to affect reality. As such, individuals' actions are often a reflection of how they feel inside. For this reason, learning to connect feelings with words and/or visuals, using words to express feelings, and practicing techniques to diffuse and manage (in the case of unwanted), or benefit from (in the case of wanted) emotions are essential skills teachers and students must practice daily. At the same time, SEL practitioners know that the language we use actively shapes and gives meaning to our and our students' experiences (Wenden, 1995). This means that the words used in our learning spaces have the potential to make classroom coexistence an enriching, positive experience or an unfavorable, upsetting memory. Consider this short vignette as an example:

> Loic, a seventh-grade student, was having a difficult day at school during his first and second periods. After lunch, Loic arrived at his third class for the day—social science.

Mr. Carranza, Loic's social science teacher, begins instruction right after the bell rings. "Sit down, everyone. The warm-up is on the board. Please remain silent as I take attendance," Mr. Carranza tells the class. Loic, filled with anxious energy from his first two classes, begins to disrupt the classroom by making noises and asking his classmates to let him borrow different things (a pencil, eraser, piece of paper, etc.). Mr. Carranza shouts in front of the class, "Loic, remember that I asked everyone to be silent. You should be working on your warm-up."

Loic, empowered by suddenly becoming the center of attention, continues to produce disruptive behaviors as a way to release the anxious energy bottled up inside. After correcting Loic a few times, Mr. Carranza loses composure, yells at Loic, and asks security to escort Loic out of the classroom. After he is escorted out of the classroom, the remaining instructional time is filled with silence, and the other students and the teacher are left with feelings of unrest, upset, or a combination of both. After social science ends, all Mr. Carranza and the other students can remember are the undesired emotions that remain within them, not the information they had reviewed in class.

THINK BOX

When presented with strong, stressful emotions, people often respond unconsciously in one of three ways: fight, flight, or freeze. These responses are often unplanned, automatic reactions each individual has that can only be controlled, or managed, through continuous, daily practice.

1. **Fight response (fight the problem):** When some individuals experience strong emotions that they are not able to manage, they externalize those feelings into strong, disruptive actions.

2. **Flight response (run away from the problem):** For some, the first unconscious reaction to overwhelming emotions is running away from them. For these individuals, running away from the problem is an act of self-preservation.

3. **Freeze response (hide from the problem):** Sometimes known as reactive or attentive immobility, freezing is a coping mechanism where individuals numb out emotions or dissociate themselves from reality to avoid the problem.

Question: Which of these three responses did Loic employ in the vignette?

Stories like Loic and Mr. Carranza's play out every day in our schools. Teachers are overwhelmed with work, and students are experiencing emotions they do not understand or know how to manage. A clash between the teacher and the student or among students occurs in the classroom, and everyone exposed to the unfortunate event is affected. Emotions of unease become the primary memories children and adults retain for the remainder of the day.

If we ask students at the end of the day, "How was school today?," chances are they will answer with an adjective that describes how they felt (their emotions), instead of the information they learned. Chances are that teachers, too, would respond to the question with an adjective that connects to a specific moment where they felt a positive or undesired emotion, instead of thinking about the content they taught that day.

Returning to Loic's example, in a learning space where SEL is practiced, Mr. Carranza might have approached Loic and kindly and discreetly ask him to accompany him outside of the classroom. Outside of class, Mr. Carranza could have asked Loic how he was feeling, not why he was misbehaving. When we ask young people "Why are you _____?" (e.g., talking, singing, misbehaving), their response will probably be "I don't know," because they truly do not understand their emotions. Instead, we should ask students how they feel; that way, students are able to vocalize their emotions and, with guidance, they will be able to connect those feelings to their actions. External actions and behaviors are a response to how students feel inside.

This practice of vocalizing feelings will help students realize that emotions externalize as actions. Some teachers might argue that this approach takes time to implement and that instruction time could suffer. However, the long-term benefits of SEL for teachers and students far outweigh not including it at all.

THINK BOX

Consider two possible long-term outcomes for Loic's example:

- Outcome #1: Mr. Carranza implements SEL practices and helps Loic understand what he is feeling and how his behavior is affecting others, and he shares some techniques on how to self-regulate those emotions and/or externalize them in a healthy manner.

  — How do you imagine Loic's future actions and school experience through the remainder of the school year as a result of this SEL practice?

  — How would Loic and Mr. Carranza's relationship evolve as a consequence of these practices?

  — How are the skills Loic learned through SEL going to help him in his life after school?

(continued)

- Outcome #2: Mr. Carranza does not implement SEL practices, continues to scold Loic and other students in front of the class when they conduct disruptive behaviors, and, if disruptive behaviors persist, asks the security to escort students out of the classroom.
  — How do you imagine Loic's future actions and school experience through the remainder of the school year as a result of this practice?
  — How would Loic and Mr. Carranza's relationship evolve as a consequence of these practices?
  — How are the skills Loic learned through scolding and getting expelled from the classroom going to help him in his life after school?

3. Your Physical (or Virtual) Learning Space Must Be Intentional

The incorporation of SEL practices needs to be both planned and intentional to be successful; it cannot be left to chance. In the same way that teachers must prepare themselves internally (i.e., mentally and emotionally) to incorporate SEL, they must also do so externally (i.e., learning space). Creating a safe and welcoming learning environment for all learners and for the teacher is key to successfully implementing SEL. As teachers and students walk into the classroom, they should feel, see, hear, and even smell a classroom culture that prioritizes social-emotional well-being.

THINK BOX

- **Physical space:** The SEL classroom should include posters that showcase classroom agreements, quick check-in boards, and a word wall explaining emotions to help students vocalize and recognize how they feel. Each teacher should design their physical space with their students in mind. Also, the physical space and the information, strategies, and ideas included on the walls should change as needed throughout the year.
- **Ambience:** When possible, play relaxing, soft instrumental or meditation music as background. The volume of this music should be soft enough that does not affect listening to others talk, but it should be loud enough that students and teachers can hear it when engaging in mindfulness activities, working individually, or completing class activities. Similarly, whenever possible, consider including plug-ins or electric oil warmers to spread soft, relaxing scents in the classroom, such as lavender or jasmine.[3] The ambiance (sense of smell and hearing) affects the students' and teachers' mood and productivity. As an important reminder, before incorporating scents into your classroom, check with your students to make sure they are comfortable with those scents and that they do not have any allergies.

(continued)

[3] For more information about essential oils and aromatherapy, please go to www.verywellmind.com/essential-oils-to-help-ease-stress-89636

- **Organization and decorations:** At the beginning of the school year, decorate your classroom, keeping in mind that choices such as color and classroom setup can affect students' first impression. For example, a traditionally arranged classroom (i.e., chairs organized in rows) might give a first impression of rigidity, whereas a classroom arranged in U shape or in groups of two or four may give students the first impression that the classroom and teacher welcome collaboration.

After reading this information, how would you organize your classroom? What specific considerations should you have based on your teaching environment? Jot down the answers to these questions, keep reading to learn more about the topic, and then return to your responses to reflect on the effectiveness of your current practices.

4. Classroom Agreements, Protocols, and Procedures Should Be Community Based

In an SEL classroom, teachers and students must first come to a consensus on guidelines—as opposed to classroom rules. For example, in your English language classroom, ask ELs at the beginning of each school year to share one or two values, guidelines, or conditions they believe are necessary for them to feel safe, welcome, and ready to learn in your classroom. Give newcomer ELs the opportunity to communicate this information in their native languages and use translation as needed. Then, as a class, find five to ten common values among all the student responses and work together to build a class poster displaying the selected common values. On the poster, write down the selected values, review all of them once again, and conduct a final vote (thumbs up or down) to agree to keep them. Throughout the year, use the classroom values to talk to your class, as a community, and redirect student behavior when students deviate from the accepted values (Pentón Herrera, 2020).

In addition to identifying guidelines, students benefit from having detailed protocols and procedures in place. For example, if you are going to start every class with 2–5 minutes of mindfulness, this practice needs to be implemented with fidelity, and nothing should jeopardize it. Knowing expectations lowers ELs' anxieties and worries and contributes to a smooth class experience for all. At the same time, in instances where students are having a difficult day or are being disruptive, a protocol and known procedures will help those students manage their emotions in an environment where they feel safe.

5. SEL Benefits From Gradual Incorporation and Consistent Application

SEL benefits from gradual incorporation, consistent application, and continuous informal assessments. Teachers who are interested in incorporating SEL into their practices for the first time should do so slowly but consistently. The key for a successful classroom implementation is finding balance—what works for one group of students might not work with another. No one expects teachers to incorporate all SEL components right away in their lesson plans and for their classroom to magically become an SEL learning environment. As you begin to incorporate SEL, remember to be kind to yourself and your students and continuously assess what is working, what is not, and what activities or resources you can incorporate to benefit you and your students.

6. School Leader and Administrator Support Is Invaluable

If your school is incorporating SEL as a schoolwide practice, your school leaders and administrators are likely familiar with expectations and have protocols set in place to promote effective SEL classroom practices. However, if your school does not engage in SEL practices, it is important to notify your school leaders and administrators of your intentions to incorporate SEL to support your ELs. School leaders must understand that some SEL practices, such as mindfulness and restorative circles, for example, are sensitive to outside interruptions. Depending on the SEL activity you are incorporating in your classroom, you may choose to post a note outside the classroom door, for example: *SEL session in progress, please do not interrupt.* Having school administrator support can directly affect how much time and space you receive for SEL in your classroom, which may affect your and your students' experiences incorporating SEL.

MEET THE TEACHER

Rochelle Knox

*English Language Development/
ESL Secondary Teacher*

*Waterloo Collegiate Institute,
Waterloo, Ontario, Canada*

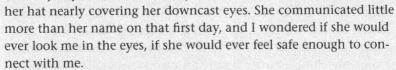

"Good morning, miss!"

I smile as I receive this greeting, remembering this student's first day in our school building. It was a cold February day and she sat silently at a table, her hat nearly covering her downcast eyes. She communicated little more than her name on that first day, and I wondered if she would ever look me in the eyes, if she would ever feel safe enough to connect with me.

If students do not feel safe, they cannot learn. Creating a safe classroom environment is even more important when students come from refugee backgrounds. All of my high school students have left their countries of origin to settle into a new country with new customs and new languages. Many of them have large gaps in their formal education and arrive in my classroom not used to sitting at a desk for long hours. Some may have never held a pencil or a book in their hands before and are now tasked with learning literacy skills, alongside the English language. Other students have lived through deeply traumatic experiences, and it is visible as the past vibrates through their bodies. At some point in their lives, all of my students have experienced feeling unsafe, sometimes even in a school setting. Therefore, before I can teach them to read, write, speak, or listen, I must attend to their social-emotional needs so that their affective filters do not get in the way of their learning.

The day begins with a friendly greeting at the door. When students enter the classroom, they sit in small groups at cooperative tables with other students at similar reading levels. This way, all students can learn at their own optimal level. On the desk in front of them, students find reading books that they can look through to help solidify past learning. Every day, we start with intention. We ground ourselves by writing the date on the board and looking out the window to check the weather. We become aware of our physical environment so that our bodies can feel present. Then, we check in with our emotional environment. This might mean talking about the news or various school events before beginning a 5-minute meditation. In this meditation, students are asked to close their eyes and bring their attention to their breathing. The simple act of silently turning our ➔

attention inward can lower cortisol levels and let our bodies know they can turn off their high alerts. I dim the lights as a physical cue to enter into a calm space. Some days, I provide coloring pages and pencil crayons so my students can give their energy an outlet.

With our intention set, our day can continue. We follow the same daily small group routine because there is safety in meeting expectations. Having my students in small groups allows me, my educational assistant, and my peer tutor to connect with students closely and show them they are valued. In groups of three to five, students often feel safer to share how they are feeling or what is happening in their lives. After a quick check-in, we begin our literacy work with readers at appropriate reading levels on subjects that are of interest to high school learners. Our rotations are never more than 25 minutes so that students can have built-in body breaks. Between rotations, students are encouraged to stand up, get a drink of water, go to the bathroom, and then participate in a class-wide activity, either a guided breathing or a yoga stretching activity. Simply lifting our arms above our heads can increase blood flow and awaken our brains. We carry tension in our bodies, especially when we have experienced trauma, so staying active can give us an outlet for stress. Though the students may not be consciously aware of it, stretching during our rotation breaks can begin to address mental health concerns.

In classes longer than 90 minutes, it is vital for us to take a body break outside the classroom. During our times outside, we sometimes play organized language games. For example, we might kick a ball back and forth in a circle and have each kicker say a word beginning with the next letter of the alphabet. Or, sometimes, when the weather is amenable, we will move our academic work to the outdoor classroom. Other times, we just walk. At these times, students are allowed to talk with each other in whatever language they choose. We give students the opportunity to connect because friendship is as important to their well-being as learning English. Many of my students feel isolated and alone, having left their communities behind in their countries of origin. After this time of connection, students return to the classroom ready to learn.

After we have read, written, and talked together, we often conclude with a game. It is important to release any tension that might have built up. Learning a language is not easy and can cause frustration. Also, students do not always learn at a steady rate. There are months when students may feel they have plateaued. Laughing together can ease these negative feelings and build classroom community. Closing on a fun note helps students take good vibes with them into the world and helps them think of English class in a positive light. There is nothing more encouraging than to have a student leave class with an enthusiastic, "See you tomorrow, miss!" ❖

In Summary

This chapter introduced the topic of SEL in English language classrooms. We discussed

- what SEL is,
- why incorporate SEL in English language teaching, and
- considerations for including SEL in your learning spaces.

We hope we have provided you in this chapter with a solid foundation of SEL and why it belongs in our ESL classrooms. Let's continue the dialogue online—there is still much more to explore. We can all learn from each other. Look for our conversation on social media using #SELforELs.

CHAPTER 2

Social-Emotional Learning in Teacher Preparation Programs

KATINA'S STORY

Katina is an instructor for a graduate program that provides teachers with certification to teach English. She shared how some groups seem easier to teach than others. Some groups participate more, seem to smile and enjoy the content more, and might even succeed in their assignments more often. For example, she said that one semester she was teaching the same exact graduate course in back-to-back time slots. The first one started at 4:30 p.m. and the second one started at 7:00 p.m. Despite her content and delivery being exactly the same for these two groups of teachers, their responses were quite different. The first group was quiet, did not seem too interested, and she had to really push for any responses from them. The 7:00 p.m. group was lively, ready to jump into conversation, and excited about pretty much anything she shared. She really did not know what was happening, so she created a survey to ask her students about their wants and needs from the course and their expectations from her in general. She also asked them to share any issues they might be having.

The earlier group had many teachers from a particular school that had experienced recent unfavorable changes in their leadership. This group of teachers would come exhausted from their day, bringing with them the negativity that was part of their school climate. Unfortunately, that feeling and energy spread across the class and affected others. The teachers in the later group came from different schools with supportive principals who wanted them to build themselves as leaders within their schools. After learning about these differences, Katina thought she would no longer teach her two classes the same way, despite it being the same course with the same objectives. She started her 4:30 p.m. group with a discussion about their day and how they got through their challenges, and they discussed how to use the content from class to help them in the future. She followed that conversation with a few minutes of in-class meditation. This practice went so well that she decided to try it with the 7 p.m. class, too. By the end of the semester, she felt such a bond with both classes that she started incorporating these mindful practices in all of her future courses.

Katina's story is not uncommon in teacher preparation programs. Teachers are human beings who are also busy, compassionate professionals. After a long day of teaching, educators may feel physically and emotionally drained, and, if not managed properly, such undesired emotions will accompany them after school. In Katina's story, the emotional toll of teaching affected the teacher preparation programs. Thankfully, however, Katina was able to find a way to uplift her students by incorporating mindfulness into her practice. Teacher educators must be aware of their students' social-emotional well-being because it will affect their classroom experience and learning.

In this chapter, we cover information about social-emotional learning (SEL) frameworks, resources, activities, and examples that you can use to prepare English language teachers.[1] You will see and reflect on how SEL can be implemented in teachers of English to speakers of other languages (TESOL) teacher education programs. We hope you find these ideas beneficial for your classes and for the TESOL educators you are training. Some ideas can be integrated into your classes quite easily as soon as tomorrow. We also offer some examples that might require more planning but are certainly worth your and your students' time.

Preparing Teachers for SEL

What should you share with your future pre- and in-service TESOL teachers? You can start with the Every Student Succeeds Act (ESSA) for some basics. Let the teachers know that, according to *English Learners and ESSA: What Educators Need to Know* (TESOL International Association, 2017), schools should spend 20% of their ESSA funding on initiatives related to the well-being of all students, such as their SEL needs. The ESSA report also points out how the SEL of English learners (ELs) and ELs with disabilities should be considered when developing language proficiency goals, because these students may have experienced a multitude of challenges.

[1] In this chapter, and throughout the book, we use *teacher preparation* to refer to university programs teaching pre- and in-service teachers as well as school counties providing teacher training/workshops to their educators.

Another important piece of background knowledge to provide would be *The 6 Principles for Exemplary Teaching of English Learners*®. Whenever possible, make connections to the principles, as they are a solid foundation for TESOL teachers to use in their daily work, starting with the importance of getting to know their students, which is very helpful for SEL:

Principle 1. Know Your Learners

Principle 2. Create Conditions for Language Learning

Principle 3. Design High-Quality Lessons for Language Development

Principle 4. Adapt Lesson Delivery as Needed

Principle 5. Monitor and Assess Student Language Development

Principle 6. Engage and Collaborate within a Community of Practice

Let your students know how there are several books/resources related to the principles: for K–12, adult education, academic and specific purposes, as well as for paraprofessionals (TESOL International Association, 2021; www.tesol.org/the-6-principles).

As introduced in Chapter 1, SEL competencies are the "essential knowledge, skills, attitudes, and mindsets that individuals need to succeed" (Taylor & Read, 2020, para. 2). Let teachers know they can embrace an SEL framework to teach social-emotional skills using evidence-based information and remind them to include stakeholders whenever possible. Also, provide teachers with appropriate resources and tools to help with SEL instruction and assessment. For example, you can share the nine frequently used frameworks (see Table 2.1) and have your students choose the one that is most applicable to their own setting (CASEL, 2020c).

You can also share with them the Measuring SEL website (measuringsel .casel.org), which provides framework briefs that expand on this information by including an overview, history, purpose and intended audience, settings, and summary for each framework. The Measuring SEL website also provides a few webinars. Table 2.1 presents the frameworks for quick comparison.

Providing teachers with resources to gain background knowledge about SEL frameworks is helpful because we know students bring with them their experiences, home cultures, values, hopes, and fears. Therefore, the more teachers know how they can bring SEL into their classes to meet their individual students' needs, the better. Focusing solely on instruction without acknowledging and caring for students' social-emotional needs ignores the students' feelings and emotions.

Table 2.1 Nine Common SEL Frameworks (CASEL, 2020c)	
SEL Framework	**Major Components**
Battelle for Kids P21 Framework	**Student Outcomes** • Key subjects and 21st-century themes • Learning and innovation skills • Information, media, and technology skills • Life and career skills
Character Lab	**Domains of Competence** • Strengths of heart—interpersonal • Strengths of will—intrapersonal • Strengths of mind—intellectual
Collaborative for Academic, Social, and Emotional Learning	**Competencies** • Self-awareness • Self-management • Social-awareness • Relationship skills • Responsible decision-making
Forum for Youth Investment	**Domains** • Emotion management • Empathy • Teamwork • Responsibility • Initiative • Problem-solving
The Habits of Mind	**Competencies** • Persisting • Thinking and communicating with clarity and precision • Managing impulsivity • Gathering data through all senses • Listening with understanding and empathy • Creating, imagining, innovating • Thinking flexibly • Responding with wonderment and awe • Thinking about thinking (metacognition) • Taking responsible risks • Striving for accuracy • Finding humor • Questioning and posing problems • Thinking interdependently • Applying past knowledge to new situations • Remaining open to continuous learning
Organization for Economic Co-operation and Development (OECD)	**Categories of Skills** • Task performance • Emotional regulation • Collaboration • Open-mindedness • Engaging with others • Compound skills (combinations of the preceding skills)

(continued on next page)

Table 2.1 (continued)

SEL Framework	Major Components
The PEAR Institute	**Elements** • Active engagement • Assertiveness • Belonging • Reflection
Search Institute	**Assets** • Internal assets—commitment to learning, positive values, social competencies, positive identity • External assets—support, empowerment, boundaries and expectations, and constructive use of time
University of Chicago's Consortium	• **Key Factors** • Agency—determining your life • Integrated identity—knowing yourself • Competencies—being able to be productive

To show your TESOL students what you mean about the importance of establishing rapport, you can model a scenario where you demonstrate how to get to know a student through questions about how they are feeling, leading into a lesson. You can demonstrate how the climate changes when you skip the friendly dialogue and simply start with a lesson.

THINK BOX

- Can you think about a time when someone approached you to ask you for something without taking the time to see how you are doing or getting to know you first?
- How did you feel?
- Why?

Jot down the answers to these questions, keep reading to learn more about the topic, and then return to your responses to reflect on the effectiveness of your current practices.

SEL in Action

Activity 1: Jigsaw

In pre- and in-service teacher programs, have your students jigsaw in person or online to learn about the different SEL frameworks. For example, break the class into groups of three and have each group learn about three SEL frameworks and then report out to the larger group (see Figure 2.1). In this way, each group only has to digest three frameworks and can, as a larger group, put together a list of similarities or differences. Students could also discuss which framework they might be more inclined to use with a particular age range and language proficiency level in mind.

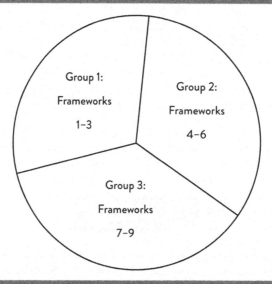

Figure 2.2 Jigsaw groups.

THINK BOX

- What other ways might you teach about the frameworks?

Jot down the answer to this question, keep reading to learn more about the topic, and then return to your response when you finish this chapter to add to your list.

MEET THE TEACHER

Stephanie Ledger

*English Language Development/
English as a Second Language
Resource Teacher*

*Waterloo Region District School
Board, Waterloo, Ontario, Canada*

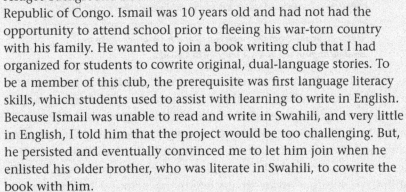

"Can I join the club?"

That was the simple but insistent
request of my student, a newcomer of
refugee background from the Democratic
Republic of Congo. Ismail was 10 years old and had not had the
opportunity to attend school prior to fleeing his war-torn country
with his family. He wanted to join a book writing club that I had
organized for students to cowrite original, dual-language stories. To
be a member of this club, the prerequisite was first language literacy
skills, which students used to assist with learning to write in English.
Because Ismail was unable to read and write in Swahili, and very little
in English, I told him that the project would be too challenging. But,
he persisted and eventually convinced me to let him join when he
enlisted his older brother, who was literate in Swahili, to cowrite the
book with him.

Soon after, Ismail and his brother worked in partnership to write
a Swahili/English book, recounting the story of their family's journey from Congo to Uganda and then Canada. When I asked Ismail
why he wanted to write a dual-language book, he explained that his
story should be written in Swahili because it was about his personal
experiences before he learned English. He did not perceive his lack
of first language literacy as a barrier, but rather a new way to recon-
nect with past experiences that were integral to his identity. As an
English as a second language (ESL) teacher, I learned a critical lesson
from my student that day. The rationale for everything that we do as
educators of ELs needs to begin with who they are, followed by how
their life story relates to their unique social-emotional needs. Only
with these insights should we begin the process of aligning students'
social-emotional and academic needs with what we teach.

Based on my experience as an ESL teacher and trainer, I recommend that educators in leadership and mentorship positions encourage their mentees to begin with listening to their students' stories,
including why they left their home countries. (E.g., was immigration
a choice or was it forced displacement?)

It is important that students have SEL opportunities, such as
accessing first language, that allow them to reflect upon and share
their life experiences. With a deeper understanding of our students →

Maisha yangu ilikua mzuri huko kwetu Congo. Lakini, kwa sababu ya vita tulilazimika kukimbia na tukakimbilia nchi ya Uganda kwenye tuliona kulikuwa amani.

My life was happy in the Congo but then there was a war. We had to leave the Congo and go to Uganda where it was safer.

Student Author: *"When I write in Swahili, I feel very proud of myself. When I came here I didn't know how to read or write ... So when my brother came to help me (write the book) I realized more and the memories keep coming back."*

This is an image from the book Ismail and his brother wrote in Swahili/English about their journey to Canada.

as individuals, we can shift our instructional paradigm from a "what-how-who sequence" (What subject-specific content and accompanying learning strategies will be taught? How will it be taught? Who will it be delivered to?) to a "who-how-what sequence" (Who are the students? How will I meet their learning needs? What strategies will I use and what content will I teach in order to meet their needs?). This shift in perspective ensures that students' background experiences, as well as their cultural and linguistic identities, are fully considered *prior* to determining instruction and assessment strategies. It prioritizes student-centered, trauma-sensitive pedagogy over the delivery of predetermined content.

As teacher mentors, we also need to send the message that students are most engaged when they can see themselves in what they are learning. Even though Ismail was not literate in Swahili, the printed code of his home language represented, and gave voice, to his identity. He benefited socially, emotionally, and academically from learning to write basic Swahili from his older brother who was able to attend school before the war. After completing their book, the brothers read their story, in both languages, to classes of students. This was an identity affirming, SEL opportunity that fostered a sense of connection for everyone involved. ❖

THINK BOX

Which SEL framework does Stephanie seem to be using in her practice? How can you tell? Would another framework have worked just as well, or better?

Activity 2: Meditation

An activity to regularly incorporate into pre- and in-service teacher programs could be meditation. At the beginning of each class (either in person or online), you can start by having everyone close their eyes—or focus on an object in the room—and think about their breathing (Gaiam, 2020). As they breathe in, you can talk about how they are breathing in energy, happy thoughts, good feelings, and a sense of relaxation. As they breathe out, you can remind them to blow out any negative feelings, issues, or problems they might be experiencing so that they can focus in class. Repeat this exercise and have your students breathe in and out slowly a few times. Each time they breathe in and out, let them know you are there to support them.

After 1–2 minutes of this meditation, start class with an engaging ice-breaker, question, or activity to get students engaged. In the ice-breaker or initial activity, you can also ask your students how these SEL activities make them feel and how they believe these practices can help their own students.

Activity 3: Scavenger Hunt

In class (either in person or online), have students break into groups and go on an online scavenger hunt for resource teachers and other support personnel their English language students might interact with regularly. Ask them how these supportive positions can connect with English language teachers to work on SEL. Then, as a class, come up with a full list of support positions available and how the individuals in those positions might help them and their ELs (socially, emotionally, academically, and otherwise). Here is a sample list:

- Reading specialist
- Special education teacher
- Speech language pathologist
- Gifted and talented teacher
- Media specialist
- Vision/hearing teachers
- Occupational therapist
- School psychologist
- School counselor
- School nurse

As an extension of the class work, you could turn this idea into a course project where teachers seek and interview each of the supports available in their schools to find out how they have connected or could connect with their school's English language teacher to work on SEL together. Let teachers know they might find that there are not too many connections occurring in their schools. However, the more support systems they can build across the institution, the better it can be for their ELs' SEL success.

MEET THE TEACHER

Nikia Darden

Elementary Reading Specialist Supporting ELs

Howard County Public Schools, Columbia, Maryland, USA

Our county decided to dedicate a week to a Black Lives Matter (BLM) curriculum across all grade levels. In the elementary level, the lessons would take place during morning circles. I was paired with a first-grade teacher to help cofacilitate the morning circles in her class. The teacher wanted her circles to be a richer experience than what the county's BLM curriculum guide was offering. As a result, she allowed me to model ways to build on the lessons to make them more robust and engaging. One lesson in particular proved to be very meaningful.

As a part of the BLM curriculum, the students were encouraged to make a piece of a quilt—simply designing the piece with colors, patterns, or pictures to display their likes and interests. We wanted to use this lesson to highlight the diverse cultures and backgrounds represented in the class. We decided to create a class culture quilt to serve as the windows and mirrors for students in the class and school community as a whole. (Windows allow students to view others' experiences, and mirrors reflect their own culture or identity in some way). I created a structured quilt piece with four sections where students could share visuals representing their favorite foods, holidays or celebrations, languages spoken in their home, and clothes they wear for special occasions. During circle time, I modeled my quilt pieces and the students made observations of the way my quilt was a window or mirror for them. In order to encourage a school-home connection, the students were given time to work on their quilt pieces at school and home. The students incorporated drawn pictures and photographs and personalized their pieces with items from home that were important to them. The pieces were beautiful, and the students were so proud!

For the next step, the teacher and I worked together to lead a gallery walk. We provided students with a pencil and clipboard to walk around and observe their classmates' work, and we created sentence frames with different levels of support for our ELs. The teacher introduced the procedure in detail—students would be given time to observe and then write about their reflections. As the students were observing their peers' quilt pieces, I modeled how to engage the students in conversation to get beyond surface level observations →

or connections. The students were so excited to learn about the different celebrations or make connections to how the same food they liked might be prepared differently in someone else's home. The quilt and the students' observations and connections were displayed in the hallway and created such a sense of pride for the students. The lesson became an experience to embrace and celebrate, teach and learn. ✛

THINK BOX

- What is the importance of connecting with resource teachers, such as reading specialists, about SEL?
- What resource teachers or personnel have you connected with to support your ELs, or which could you?
- How can (or has) this connection focused on SEL work for you and your ELs?

Jot down the answers to these questions, keep reading to learn more about the topic, and then return to your responses to reflect on the effectiveness of your current practices.

Activity 4: Walk the Walk

When planning activities for classes, try to actively engage students with strategies that they, in turn, should use with their own students. That way, they learn objectives in some of the similar ways that they would teach their ELs. It also gives teachers some perspective from the students' standpoints.

For the walk the walk activity, set up the classroom similar to a poster session at a conference, where pairs work together to create a poster with their ideas to formally present to peers as they walk around the space. Because the focus is on SEL for ELs, have each pair share how and why they would use an SEL activity in their class. Some examples:

- The poster shows how a teacher could include some yoga poses after a writing activity to allow students to stretch their bodies and relax their minds after having responded to a writing prompt, which might be challenging for ELs, depending on their proficiency level.
- The poster displays information about teaching vocabulary related to emotions, because ELs could benefit from developing their vocabulary to express how they are feeling in English (Cherry, 2020). It includes having students complete a list-group-label activity where they cluster together emotions by category and create labels/headings for their groupings, such as happiness, sadness, and fear.

Students really enjoy the walk the walk activity, especially when they learn how they can potentially present their poster ideas at conferences. This takes the activity to a higher level, because it can be shared with colleagues, in addition to their own students. Teachers also enjoy learning about ideas from each other.

Once the posters are complete, have half of the class walk around while the other half presents their posters. Remind them how activities similar to this one make presenting less threatening for our ELs, while providing them with time to practice their writing and speaking skills. At the end of the poster session, ask teachers how they would feel if you had them do the presentation in front of the whole group. Then ask them to raise their hands if they prefer the poster session to the traditional presentation. You will note that most (if not everyone) raise their hand.

Integrating Technology

We are using technology now more than ever for our classrooms. Many courses are fully online, while some remain hybrid or face-to-face. Regardless of the method of instruction, finding the right balance of what to use to benefit students, rather than to just say we are using technology for the sake of using technology, can be a struggle for some teachers. Using the International Society for Technology in Education (ISTE) standards can help teachers learn, lead, collaborate, design, and facilitate online instruction. The ISTE standards demonstrate the importance of goal-setting, problem-solving, and assessing goals (International Society for Technology in Education, 2017).

Useful Tech Tools: Video Editing and Screencasting

Software that allows you to edit videos and other presentation media and then screencast to share with students can be extremely useful and beneficial. There are a number of software platforms that accomplish this, such as the following:

- Prezi (prezi.com)
- Camtasia (www.techsmith.com/video-editor.html)
- Open Broadcaster Software (obsproject.com)
- Screencast-O-Matic (screencast-o-matic.com)

Screencast-O-Matic (2019) is our favorite; this resource allows you to place a PowerPoint or other visual online while you video record yourself providing an explanation, including captions if you wish. Teachers may stop or replay parts of the video if they need. Screencast-O-Matic can make a PowerPoint with no sound—or just a voiceover without a video—come to life. It also helps create lessons for the days you might be asynchronous and want teachers to view your presentation to discuss later, such as in a flipped classroom. Here is an example of a presentation we created for a group of teachers called "English Learners with Dyslexia": www.youtube.com/watch?v=5bT5xZDF-3Y. As you will see, even though it is a static video, we used questions throughout and paused for teachers to think about potential answers, which we followed up by providing answers.

Screencast-O-Matic can also be a nice way for teachers to have ELs create class presentations at home, without having to talk in front of an entire group. ELs can take their time making their Screencast-O-Matic presentations and can share the final product after revising and editing their work. It can also be a good way for English language teachers to provide backup directions to assignments that students can look over after class. As you know, assignments sometimes make sense when a teacher explains them in class but, once students get home, they might not remember all of the details. As a result, this resource can help alleviate some stress for students.

Useful Tech Tools: Writing Online

Another goodie for you to use in teacher education classes are websites for writing online, which can help with visual brainstorming, explain difficult or complex processes, and turn text-heavy content into a visual story, among other things to ease stress. A few programs to consider:

- Thinkglink (www.thinglink.com)
- Piktochart (piktochart.com)
- Glogster (edu.glogster.com)
- Smore (www.smore.com/teachers)

Smore (2020) is our software of choice to write online: You can provide news, tips, themed content related to SEL, guessing games to create an engaging environment (see Figure 2.2), among other things on a Smore. Smores are great for ELs who cannot write extended responses and need visuals to help with comprehension. It is fun and easy to create one of these posters. Walk the walk, as we talked about earlier, and find ways to use the technology in your class, and let teachers know how they in turn can use it in theirs.

Figure 2.2 Smore poster: Who am I?

Lesson Planning With SEL

Having a clear template to plug in objectives and steps while integrating SEL into lesson plans reminds teachers to look beyond the language proficiency development they are working on with their students. The following outline can be tweaked to meet individual teachers' needs, but provides a base for ideas to think about when planning.

Example Template for Lesson Planning With SEL

- Language Objectives (e.g., reading, writing, listening, speaking):

- Content Objectives:

- SEL Core Competencies (from Chapter 1: self-awareness, self-management, social awareness, relationship skills, responsible decision-making):

- Materials (e.g., texts, websites, apps to help meet the objectives):

- Procedure (items to consider):
    a. integrating SEL into part of the lesson or throughout the lesson
    b. using small groups to help students feel comfortable talking and sharing their work with peers
    c. using technology to aid with instruction
    d. including culturally responsive materials/texts
    e. differentiating to meet needs of different language proficiency levels

- Assessment (items to consider):
    a. assessing language and SEL core competencies
    b. differentiating by providing options for assignments and projects when applicable

Another factor to consider when lesson planning is home-school connections. Share how reaching out to family members provides families with a voice and can also provide teachers with ideas for ways their students can learn at home. Making that home-school connection helps caregivers feel valued, and working together can have a positive effect on all parties. In addition, sharing with caregivers methods used for instruction can help them understand how they might incorporate learning strategies at home (Schlund et al., 2020).

ADDITIONAL RESOURCE

For more detailed information on how to develop and include SEL objectives, see the following:

Yoder, N., & Dusenbury, L. (2017). *A process for developing and articulating learning goals or competencies for social and emotional learning.* American Institutes for Research, and Collaborative for Academic, Social, and Emotional Learning. casel.org/wp-content/uploads/2017/02/Process_Developing_Articulating_Learning_Goals_final-2-22-17.pdf

MEET THE TEACHER

Mamiko Nakata

Lecturer

Hitotsubashi University, Tokyo, Japan

I train preservice teachers to incorporate SEL's key skills into daily classroom routines and after-school programs, just as I used them in my own teaching practice in secondary English language classes several years ago.

Every EL can benefit from learning prosocial behaviors and enhancing their ability to succeed in school, careers, and life. I have summarized two areas I'd like to focus on next.

Reading Materials

Contemporary fiction and essential nonfiction (e.g., biographies), such as Penguin Graded Readers written for ELs, are great sources of social-emotional learning. These books, having the language level simplified and graded for vocabulary, grammar structures, and the number of words, are a wonderful resource for teaching character traits, feelings, and actions. By using these books, ELs of all levels can learn to identify, label, and express their emotions. They also provide opportunities for teaching about social situations and emotion identification and regulation. ELs will learn to relate with the characters and internalize lessons as well. In all the years I taught secondary level ELs and of all the books I used, surprisingly, advanced ELs loved and sympathized the most with Buck, part St. Barnard and part Scottish Shepherd, in *The Call of the Wild*!

Character Education (School-Wide Practices)

School-wide practices and activities also create opportunities for students' voice and autonomy and build a sense of community. My former middle school had character education embedded in morning announcements. Each week, a "virtue of the week" was introduced by the guidance counselor using an anecdote. Then, a daily prompt was given and students were supposed to write a short journal entry. Throughout the day, staff encouraged students to practice the virtue. By having this practice implemented school-wide, everyone could work together on exercising these virtues, which helped my ELs understand them better. ❖

- What are some SEL practices you want to focus on?

Jot down the answer to this question, keep reading to learn more about the topic, and then return to your response to add to or revise your list.

Teacher Stress Reduction

What are some ways that ESOL teachers can get stressed? There are many, but following are a few that a focus group in one of my (Gilda's) classes shared:

- Helping students with assessments
- Completing paperwork
- The responsibility of knowing ELs' stories
- The responsibility of helping students succeed academically and in life
- Lack of time for self-care

Are you educating your teachers about the importance of self-care and well-being? For example, talking about the importance of regularly exercising? Exercising regularly might mean going on walks to help with mood and energy. How about sleep? Are you talking to teachers about keeping a schedule that includes how many hours they plan to sleep? As teacher educators, it is vital to share with teachers how having a schedule can help ensure they take time for self-care. Other things to keep in mind include diet, amount of time watching the news, and relationships. Remember we all need balance, so make sure you discuss this information with your teachers (Bertin, 2020). Start now by creating a realistic schedule for yourself in a calendar that includes your own SEL activities, if you have not done so already.

Sample Day

6:00 a.m.	Breakfast (oatmeal or something healthy and filling)
6:30 a.m.	Yoga stretches
7:00 a.m.	Commute to work (listening to podcasts focusing on positive messages)
8:00 a.m.	Teach (include meditation with students)
12:00 p.m.	Lunch (with an effort to eat healthy)
12:30 p.m.	Teach (include meditation with students)
3:00 p.m.	Walk outside

4:00 p.m.	Grading/planning/reflection/seeking support
6:00 p.m.	Dinner (again trying to eat healthy, including vegetables)
10:00 p.m.	Sleep

As you can see, keeping a routine to help you stay healthy both mentally and physically does not need to be complicated. Sharing the importance of self-care and well-being with teachers is critical in helping with teacher retention and avoiding teacher burnout. Many teachers leave the profession because they do not get the support they need or do not know how to find balance during their first years of teaching. Help your teachers by letting them know it is okay to take time to recharge and that they should not feel guilty about it. Read Chapter 3 for more information about teacher self-care and well-being.

THINK BOX

- Are you talking to your teachers about self-care and well-being?
- What is working?
- What can be improved?
- How are your teachers reacting to this knowledge?

Jot down the answers to these questions, keep reading to learn more about the topic, and then return to your responses to reflect on the effectiveness of your current practices.

In Summary

This chapter provides many ideas to think about and use in TESOL teacher education programs, whether they are preservice or in-service programs. We discussed:

1. A brief overview of the SEL evidence base to share with teachers
2. Nine common SEL frameworks with a jigsaw activity to use to help learn them
3. How to incorporate meditation into classes along with an example
4. A scenario and activity about connecting with support personnel, such as reading specialists
5. Using a conference poster session format to present SEL activities
6. How to integrate technology to help alleviate student stress
7. Components to include in SEL lesson plans
8. How to share with teachers the importance of planning for their own stress reduction

The activities shared throughout this chapter can be used by English language teachers for any grade or language proficiency level with accommodations based on student needs. Show teachers how the activities can be modified so that they are able to review any lesson or resource and see how it might possibly work for their students with some adjustments. We hope we have provided you with much food for thought for your teacher education programs. Let's continue the dialogue online—there is still much more to explore. We can all learn from each other. Look for our conversation on social media, using #SELforELs.

CHAPTER 3

Teacher Self-Care and Well-Being

TAKERU'S STORY

During his first year of teaching English as a new language, Takeru had a difficult time finding balance to meet all the school demands and supporting his newcomer English learners (ELs) with different situations that extended beyond teaching English, such as helping them fill out school lunch forms and searching for community organizations who could support the costs of students' required vaccinations. The first year of teaching left Takeru drained and questioning his effectiveness as a language educator. Now in his second year of teaching English to newcomers, Takeru began the school year determined to continue supporting his ELs, thinking that the previous year had equipped him with the necessary knowledge needed to deal with any situation that came his way.

During the first couple of months, the school year seemed to be going smoothly. Students were quickly grasping the content taught, and there were few issues with student behavior or any other concerns. In particular, Felipe, one of the ELs, was showing much promise. Felipe was a 19-year-old newcomer who arrived alone to reunite with his mother after 10 years of separation. During the beginning of the school year, Felipe showed excitement to be learning English in school and was always willing and ready to help his classmates. The first progress report showed that Felipe was on his way to receiving excellent grades in all of his classes, which would earn him an award for excellent academic performance. Takeru congratulated Felipe and other students who earned excellent marks in front of the class with a big round of applause and a modest celebration.

During the next couple of months, however, Takeru witnessed a quick decline in Felipe's school participation and academic performance. Takeru did not know that Felipe was currently living with his mother and her alcoholic husband, someone Felipe did not know prior to arriving in this new country. The stepfather, when he got drunk, would often physically attack Felipe's mother, and, eventually, he also began attacking Felipe. The situation that Felipe was experiencing at home was affecting his grades and academic performance. Felipe could not focus on school because his mind was often wandering around to escape his reality.

Seeing Felipe's quick academic decline, Takeru initially suspected that something was not okay at home, but when he called Felipe's mother, the phone number that appeared in the student's records did not work. One day, Takeru's suspicions were sadly confirmed when Felipe arrived in class with bruises on his arm and neck. Seeing this, Takeru quickly called the school's nurse, social worker, and counselor, and measures were taken. Takeru had done what he was supposed to do, and the school system was trying to respond to Felipe's needs.

Regardless of the steps taken by Takeru and the school's social worker and counselor, Felipe continued to dissociate from school and eventually stopped attending. When Felipe dropped out, Takeru felt a deep sense of guilt and regret. He kept asking himself what he could have done differently to help Felipe or how he could have supported Felipe differently in their classroom. Takeru's sense of guilt continued to build throughout the remainder of the school year and was further compounded by undesired emotions resulting from different events that occurred to other newcomers. Takeru's inability to regulate his sense of guilt and other undesired emotions began to percolate into his teaching practice and personal life. Eventually, a feeling of helplessness took a toll on Takeru's mental and emotional well-being, leaving him overwhelmed, mentally drained, and emotionally exhausted for the remainder of the school year.

Takeru's story is, unfortunately, not uncommon for teachers. As we know, teaching is one of the most rewarding and demanding professions, and in most cases, it becomes our way of life. Many educators would agree that when we commit ourselves to our profession, the lines between our professional world and our personal lives blur, and we often take home the feelings and emotions we carry with us from our teaching. Teacher well-being is rarely emphasized in education contexts presently, but well-being is the most important element for our practice as educators, our students' success, and the school environment. In this chapter, we emphasize teacher self-care and well-being as foundational requirements for providing ELs with social-emotional learning (SEL) opportunities.

Taking Care of Ourselves

You can start the important task of taking care of yourself by logging what you are currently doing in your daily routine to see where SEL activities might fit best for you. You will be the one working on them, so the activities really need to fit with your lifestyle and schedule. Remember not to feel guilty about taking time for yourself. SEL for your own well-being is like being on an airplane when the flight attendant tells you to put on your oxygen mask before putting it on your child. You need to be able to take care of your well-being first in order to take care of someone else. Your ELs need you; make sure you are cared for so that you can care for them. Here is an example of a day prior to making time for SEL activities:

> **" YOUR ELS NEED YOU; MAKE SURE YOU ARE CARED FOR SO THAT YOU CAN CARE FOR THEM. "**

6:00 a.m.	Coffee
7:00 a.m.	Commute to work (listen to the news while eating a peanut butter sandwich)
8:30 a.m.	Teach (include meditation with students)
12:00 p.m.	Lunch (bagel with cream cheese)
12:30 p.m.	Teach (include meditation with students)
3:00 p.m.	Grading/planning/reflection
6:00 p.m.	Dinner (pick up a pizza or other takeout)
10:00 p.m.	Sleep

As you saw in Chapter 2, by reflecting on your day, you can make time to add in some important SEL practices, such as eating oatmeal for breakfast at home, doing some yoga stretches, listening to positive podcasts, eating healthier, walking, and seeking support rather than working on your own entirely. The difference in the amount of time it takes for SEL is not huge, but the transformation in how you feel can be. Getting an SEL routine going, such as the sample in Chapter 2, includes all of the SEL core competencies. It also includes Principle 6 from TESOL's 6 Principles, "engage and collaborate within a community of practice" (TESOL International Association, 2021), where teachers collaborate with each other for support to develop instruction, get ideas, and become more engaged in their work.

Following are a number of activities that you can add to your daily routine to help you improve your well-being, often while also working on your students' as well.

SEL in Action

Activity 1: Journaling With Balance

If you enjoy writing, start a journal about your reflections. Reflect on your own SEL practices, in addition to how you include those in your English language classroom. You can easily create overlap so that you can work on your students' SEL while working on your own. For example, if you notice that you and your students get frustrated when people speak out of turn, how can you work on improving that? Write down some ideas in your reflection journal. Perhaps you can role-play appropriate turn taking with your students for them to see what it looks like. You can talk to them about how it makes people feel when they are interrupted while trying to speak. This can be true while talking online in video chats, too. It is especially easy to talk over people on a Zoom call, for example. However, by modeling how to say something like, "Sorry, please finish your thoughts and then I will share mine," you can help students learn how to be courteous, and everyone can have a conversation without feeling frustrated. For ELs, who have to think carefully about what they are going to say in English, interruptions can shut them down completely, so addressing interruptions can be very helpful to their emotional health.

In the journal, list one or two things that frustrate you each day, and then a positive way to work through them the next time. Then, as you try out the ideas, journal about them to note your own progress. Do not forget to list one or two positive things from each day for balance. In time, you might note that overall you are thinking more positively about how you can make things work, rather than simply feeling frustrated. You can also have your students journal about their reflections at the end of each class, so you can all do it together. The practice of journaling can incorporate all of the SEL core competencies, depending on what you need or want to reflect on each day, and can also align with Principle 1 ("know your learners") and Principle 2. ("create conditions for language learning") from *The 6 Principles for Exemplary Teaching of English Learners*®.

THINK BOX

- How else might you journal to engage in SEL?

Jot down the answer to this question, keep reading to learn more about the topic, and then return to your response to reflect on the effectiveness of your current practices and to add more journaling ideas.

Activity 2: Peer Connections

It is very easy to get stuck in a routine where you work, work, and work trying to cover all of your objectives during class, planning outside of class, and rushing through chores once home, telling yourself you do not have time to connect with peers. Yet, when we do take the time to connect with peers, we feel refreshed. We can talk through our stumbling blocks, and we can hear about others' stumbling blocks. Have you ever found that when you talk to someone else about your issues, you realize your issues are similar or maybe even not as bad?

With other English language teachers, you can help develop your students' SEL experiences together, sharing ideas for activities or lessons. And, with other English language teachers, you can also develop your own SEL experiences and practices. For example, you can go on a walk with a peer. In addition to a walk being time to exercise, move the body, and help with stress by detaching from our work spaces (at home, in school or school buildings), walking with a peer can make the entire experience even better. You might also find yourself ready to come back to work with renewed energy. Or, you might find that you like to talk to your peers without the walk. Make it work for you; that is the key. This practice can incorporate all of the SEL core competencies, depending on what you (or your students) need or want to get out of the peer connections, and it can work on Principle 6 ("engage and collaborate within a community of practice") from *The 6 Principles for Exemplary Teaching of English Learners®*.

MEET THE TEACHER

Ethan Trinh

English to Speakers of Other Languages Instructor and PhD Student

Georgia State University, Atlanta, Georgia, USA

Dear Colleagues,
As I write this message to you, I realize I have been sitting in front of my computer, checking and responding to emails, for most of the day. I understand we are all busy with paperwork, grading, students' and families' inquiries, the school's new plan, so on and so forth. We get stuck in our chairs, desks, or couches, especially during the global pandemic.

Let's pause for a moment and take a deep breath. That's what I am doing now. Let's do it together. Let's take a deep breath, inhale, and exhale deeply. Listen to the sound in your chest. Let's do it one more time. I cannot emphasize enough how important it is for us, teachers, to be mindful of our breathing as we stare at the computer screen for too long, and the emails keep clogging our inbox. We take a deep breath to remind us that the emails can wait to be responded to, and that we need to give ourselves a moment . . . for a deep breath. ➜

I am preparing a lesson on the difference between "House" and "Home" for my English language class. I am excited about the engagement and laughter that they will have. But, I also need to take care of household chores and reorganize the mess on my desk. I need to make my desk home for me. I need to make this space a place for me to breathe, think, (re)energize, and find inspiration when I come to work every day. Every time I get stuck, I clean up my working corner because I feel I am being taken care of. I play a list of random songs and reorganize my space. I am reorganizing myself and other things stuck in my head.

Now that we have taken a moment to breathe deeply and organize our physical space, let's take a walk together. I always try to get some sunlight, despite the cold weather in my state right now. But walking together is a way to connect with each other and connect with ourselves. By walking, we find a space to think deeply about our problems. We need space to pull things together. Or, at least, we need space to listen to our bodies. We are walking meditatively. We take a deep breath. We reorganize our messes. We come back with a ready-to-fight spirit. We remember that we need to take care of ourselves first.

Thank you for your mindful practices, your spatial cleanup, and your walking meditation. That's what I have been doing to take care of myself while tackling anxiety and stress, and teaching my ELs. ✢

THINK BOX

Ethan needed to take time for self-care.

- How often do you remind yourself to take time for self-care?
- What does self-care look like for you?

Jot down the answer to these questions, keep reading to learn more about the topic, and then return to your responses to reflect on the effectiveness of your current practices.

Activity 3: Zoom Room

Ethan shared how reorganizing a desk can be a part of self-care; organizing your Zoom room can also be a part of self-care. By now, you have probably heard of ways to make your Zoom room (or online home teaching environment) better. For example, you can

- make sure the camera is looking down on you slightly (this is considered the most flattering camera angle),
- connect a microphone for optimal sound, and
- make sure the lighting is sufficient.

Let's take this to the next level. Have you heard about Room Rater (n.d.)? It is on Twitter @ratemyskyperoom, and by looking through it you can see how people rate others' online meeting rooms, many of which are newscasters' rooms at home. It turns out that by including a plant and art, room ratings increase. You might be asking yourself: How does this relate to self-care? Well, if you take the time to organize a room that provides you peace every time you have to work in it, you are indeed engaging in practices that contribute to your well-being. Take a look at the Zoom room in Figure 3.1 and Figure 3.2, before and after having taken the time to make it more peaceful.

Figure 3.1 Zoom room before.

Figure 3.2 Zoom room after.

You might think having a bookshelf in your background makes you look like you are ready to work. How does it make you feel, though? In this Zoom room example, the camera was simply moved to the other side of the room, and some art and a plant were incorporated.

The feeling of the room went from being overwhelming with a crowded bookshelf in the background to feeling tidy and organized. If you do not have a room in your house where you teach, you can always find a plain wall to put behind you and try to incorporate a plant on the side and/or some art. If you have to spend all day looking at it, the image should make you feel good.

You will likely notice that some people opt for virtual backgrounds to conceal their rooms, which can work too. If you cannot (or do not want to) organize a space, you might enjoy being in a different country each day. Pick your students' home countries to show yourself in as you teach, and change them regularly so you can go around the world. Regardless of whether you organize your physical space or go virtual, try to make a background that helps you feel good every time you have to look at it. This practice can help build the SEL core competency of self-awareness and aligns with Principle 1 ("know your learners") and Principle 2 ("create conditions for language learning") from *The 6 Principles for Exemplary Teaching of English Learners®*.

Activity 4: Self-Care Icebreaker

Next time you are leading a workshop or are teaching, start with an icebreaker where everyone shares one way they are taking time for self-care (CASEL, 2020d). If it is online, use this activity as a warm-up where people type their responses in the chat box while they wait for you to get started. Provide some examples, and tell them if they are not doing any activities for their well-being at the moment, they can list something they would like to do in the future.

It can be interesting to know what everyone is practicing for self-care, and it also starts your time with students on a positive note, where everyone can share one highlight from their self-care strategies. Read through the different ideas and celebrate how students are taking time for self-care. Here is a summary of a self-care list generated from a recent workshop:

- Adopting a pet
- Starting to exercise (yoga, bike riding, jumping rope, paddle boarding, etc.)
- Taking time to cook
- Watching "feel good" movies
- Participating in community circles (safe spaces to share feelings or thoughts)
- Connecting with peers through Zoom
- Birdwatching

You might find that you can connect with others based on similar interests after seeing the list that is generated by your group. For example, someone from the example list shared they are birdwatching; if that is something you like to do as well, you can connect with them on a personal level. Learn from each other. (In this particular workshop, the student later shared that you can learn about bird counts from all over the world on the Cornell website [www.birds.cornell.edu/home/citizen-science-be-part-of -something-bigger], the teacher used this resource as an opportunity to have students share about birds from their countries. As a self-care activity, birdwatching can be a great excuse to get outside and enjoy nature or simply look out your window to see what you can see while taking a break.)

This icebreaker practice can help build the SEL core competency of self-awareness and relationship skills, and it aligns with Principle 1 ("know your learners") and Principle 2 ("create conditions for language learning") from *The 6 Principles for Exemplary Teaching of English Learners®*.

Help Yourself

Activity 5: There's an App for That

There are many apps for self-care and well-being. For example, on Chopra's 21-Day Meditation Experience, you get a message for the day and a reflection prompt. In addition, Oprah Winfrey and Deepak Chopra narrate 20-minute meditations. You might find reading the message of the day and reflecting on it using their prompt to be rewarding. If you are so inclined, you can also pay for unlimited access, music, and other features.

Ask your peers about apps they might be using for self-care and well-being. There are many available for teachers and students. Some have excellent visuals and simple text that can help ELs, some are focused on grade ranges (such as early childhood or adolescents), while some provide a game format. Find the one that works for you, to either remind you to take time for self-care or to help you build your own SEL skills.

Activity 6: Learn to Say No

Do you love saying yes? Do people ask you for favors to take on more work, to be on a new committee, among other things, and you find yourself always saying yes? Perhaps you enjoy interacting with people, so you figure that these additional experiences will provide you with more opportunities to engage. Alternatively, perhaps you just do not know how to say no without feeling guilty—saying no can be difficult, and it can be considered an art. At some point, you need to say no. When we always say yes, work starts to pile up and we can become overstretched and overwhelmed. Some suggestions for letting people down easy include letting them know you

- have prior scheduling conflicts,
- are at capacity with projects, or
- need a skillset further developed to do the task.

(OfficeNinjas, 2020)

As far as your students go, you might find that they (depending on their home countries and previous experiences) do not know the proper boundaries between a teacher and a student. For example, ELs might ask teachers to print out their reports for their classes because they did not have time to buy ink for their printer. Some students might even feel entitled to this service. Also, parents might ask a teacher to come to their house after school to tutor their child in a demanding way. In circumstances like these, teachers need to take a step back and reflect on how best to handle the *no*. In the end, you are doing the asker a favor because it can only help them in the future to know what is and is not appropriate to ask of a teacher.

Afterward, you can follow up with them to check on how things are going and help them in other ways that are appropriate, such as helping the student plan their daily routine or directing them to tutoring resources. They will realize you do want to help them, even if it is within limits. In the end, saying no (with a supportive explanation) can lead others to understand how you can help them. This practice can help build all of the SEL core competencies and aligns with Principle 1 ("know your learners") and Principle 2 ("create conditions for language learning") from *The 6 Principles for Exemplary Teaching of English Learners*®.

Embrace Yourself

With all of the opportunities for online workshops and conferences these days, you might be able to attend a variety of professional development opportunities related to self-care. You might find tips that make you pause and reflect, such as reminding yourself that:

1. Your emotional health is of utmost importance.
2. You should not judge how you are coping based on how others are coping.
3. You should not judge how others are coping based on how you are coping.

(Jara, 2020)

We really do need to reflect on what we can do and not worry about comparing ourselves to others. Do you compare yourself to others? Remind yourself that we are not in a competition. We need to work through life as best we can, and that will look different for each person. This is especially true for our students, coming from different countries, with different concerns that may or may not overlap with each other. Embrace yourself and encourage your students to do the same.

CARLOS'S STORY: NOW WHAT?

Carlos lives alone because his only child recently moved out. You might think going from one to none is easy, but it has been very hard for him as a Latino because in his culture, family means everything. He finds himself lonely and wanting to talk to his daughter, but he cannot call her every day for a long chat. She is busy "adulting" or working on being on her own. He looks at others with young children and thinks back on how it used to be with her as a young child. He was always taking her places, playing games at home, and sharing meals. The question for him is, "Now what?"

Carlos has decided to focus on his career, considering what the next phase of his life might look like, and he is trying to take steps often to work toward his goals. He has a vision board with some goals, which include keeping close to family, traveling, exercising, and, of course, working. Revisiting the "Now what?" question on a regular basis has helped him readjust goals for his social-emotional well-being.

Regardless of where you are in life, whether you have children, or where you are in your career trajectory, the question of "now what?" could be brewing for you, too. In the same way revisiting this question has helped Carlos, it can also help you figure out what is working in your life and what you might need to shift.

How is your life changing? How is your teaching career going? What are your next steps? This is an activity that we can also share with our students, to help them learn to set life goals and learn to readjust through events and time. Our ELs might be focused on simply getting through each day because of their recent arrival in the country. Helping them look ahead can be inspirational and can assist them in learning about the steps necessary to succeed. You can help mentor them through goals—after taking care of your goals first. (Remember, this chapter is all about teacher self-care and well-being because it is so very important that you take the time to focus on yourself first.)

THINK BOX

- What does "now what?" look like for you?
- How will you include this question in class for your students to reflect on?

Activity 7: Me Time

Earlier, we discussed how peer connections can improve your mood and help with your self-care routine. You might, however, find that you need "me time" after (or even instead of) peer connections. Maybe walks work best for you while alone to recharge yourself. Self-care is about what *you* need, which might look different for each of us.

Deep Breathing

One practice you can engage in as part of "me time" is to do deep breathing exercises. Special deep breathing GIFs are available to help set the rhythm, such as those on the Destress Monday website (www.mondaycampaigns .org/destress-monday/6-gifs-to-help-you-relax): These animated images consist of a shape expanding and contracting to help you time your inhalations and exhalations. The visuals can be very helpful to get into the zone of relaxing and taking deep breaths. And, the GIFs can be used by your students as well because they do not require any language proficiency to follow along.

Reading and Viewing

For "me time" entertainment, you might enjoy sitting with a cup of coffee while reading a book of interest. Or, you might like taking time on your own to watch your favorite shows on television. For example, watching a feel-good show can help you detach from day-to-day routines, immerse in a culture, and have a few laughs. Try not to get caught up in books or television shows that drag you down. There are many deep, dark, and interesting books, shows, and movies that you might find very thought provoking, but for the purposes of self-care and mood improvement, those might not be the best choices. Note how you feel after reading or watching certain genres and choose wisely during your "me time," so you end up feeling refreshed—and not depressed. You can talk to your students about favorite genres and get suggestions from each other, a conversation that can help widen your reading and viewing habits and also build rapport with students.

Self-Pampering

Another way to enjoy "me time" is to self-pamper. Try applying a face mask made of honey. This reduces thinking time and allows you to just relax while you give yourself your own personal spa time.

Most important, make "me time" all about you, and if you can find ways to make "me time" connections with students, it is an added bonus. This practice can help build the SEL core competency of self-awareness, and also aligns with Principle 1 ("know your learners") from *The 6 Principles for Exemplary Teaching of English Learners*®.

MEET THE TEACHER

Tina Ruiz

English to Speakers of Other Languages Educational Specialist

Baltimore City Public Schools, Baltimore, Maryland, USA

Nearing a year into a pandemic, self-care has never been more important and more challenging. Two months into the pandemic, I moved into a new position in my school district with new responsibilities. Managing a career move in "unprecedented times" can definitely heighten stress, and self-care is easy to put on the back burner.

As a single mom of two teenage boys, my self-care routine prior to the pandemic revolved around the hustle and bustle of parenting duties. Fitting in a barre class during my son's 45-minute band practice or dropping my older son off at tae kwon do and running 30 minutes in the neighborhood surrounding the *dojang*. Suddenly, neither son was going to band practice or tae kwon do, and the barre studio closed for in-person workouts. More and more, I found myself ending the night exhausted, trying to adjust to my new normal—including a new job— without an outlet. I was burning out and I needed to make a change.

The pandemic had caused all of my priorities to already dramatically shift. Taking the opportunity to rethink how to take care of myself didn't seem novel, rather just a natural adaptation in a changing time. I signed up for virtual races and skipped the Chardonnay on weeknights in order to wake up and do a virtual high-intensity interval training class in my basement before my 8 a.m. Zoom meeting. Today, I'm feeling stronger and less frenzied, and I have some awesome new race medals from virtual 5Ks! ✥

Activity 8: Self-Care Gifts

Have you given yourself any gifts lately? You might consider your own self-care basket. It might not need to be an actual basket, but giving yourself occasional gifts to promote your self-care can be fun. Maybe a gift to yourself is getting a new app for meditation. Or, maybe you find a shea butter cream that smells very relaxing and helps you feel less anxious. You could get a foot massager to help pamper your feet after being on them all day. (Foot massagers also help with blood circulation, so they are good if you sit all day, too.) Another idea is to get a foam back roller, which looks like a wide noodle; this can help you stretch out your back when it gets stiff from working on the computer too long. Treat yourself to a quick backstretch, so you can get back to work feeling less tense.

Take a minute to think about what makes you tense, and how you might give yourself a gift to help combat that. Once again, talk to your colleagues to see what kinds of things they buy for themselves to relax. You can also find out from your students what typical items are used in their home countries for relaxation to try out some of those ideas (and you can even make a lesson out of this). Remember, you need to actively take care of yourself with what makes sense for you. Just make sure to find what is right for you to improve your well-being and make a conscious effort to regularly do it.

Activity 9: Do Nothing

Sometimes, the best thing we can do for our own well-being is to do nothing. Just sit around, relax, eat, take a nap, and take time off from the screens (social media, television, video games, etc.). Give yourself permission to do nothing. Do not feel guilty. You will reap the rewards the next day when you feel renewed because you have given your mind and body a break from your daily routine. As the Italians say, *il dolce far niente*, or: *the sweetness of doing nothing* can be very enjoyable (Beard, 2019).

As a teacher of ELs, not only do you plan carefully to meet language and content objectives, but you also plan for the things that are not part of the plan. For example, you try to foresee how students might react (or not react) based on their backgrounds, struggles, and English/academic proficiency levels. This is a lot to plan for, to consider, and to think about. You deserve a break! Know that by letting yourself do nothing, you will actually be better prepared to help your students in the long run. At work, this might translate into doing nothing during your lunch breaks. Just eat and relax rather than multitasking. And, remind your students that they, too, should take breaks. This practice can help build the SEL core competencies of self-awareness, self-management, and responsible decision-making, and can give you the energy needed to develop the 6 Principles once you are back at work.

ADDITIONAL RESOURCE

For more information about self-care, see the following:

Waterford.org. (2021). *Why teacher self-care matters and how to practice self-care in your school.* www.waterford.org/education /teacher-self-care-activities

---

In Summary

This chapter provides many ideas to think about and use for teacher self-care and well-being. We discussed the following:

1. Journaling with balance
2. Utilizing peer connections
3. Improving your Zoom room
4. Implementing a self-care icebreaker to learn ideas and connect with others
5. Apps for self-care
6. The art of saying no
7. Embracing yourself (by not judging coping methods)
8. Asking yourself "Now what?" and readjusting goals
9. Making time for "me time"
10. Self-care gifts
11. Doing nothing (truly taking a mental and physical break)

The activities shared throughout this chapter can be used by all teachers, but the explanations around them demonstrate how teachers of ELs can connect with their students and their families to provide themselves with self-care. Let's continue the dialogue online—there is still much more to explore. We can all learn from each other. Look for our conversation on social media using #SELforELs.

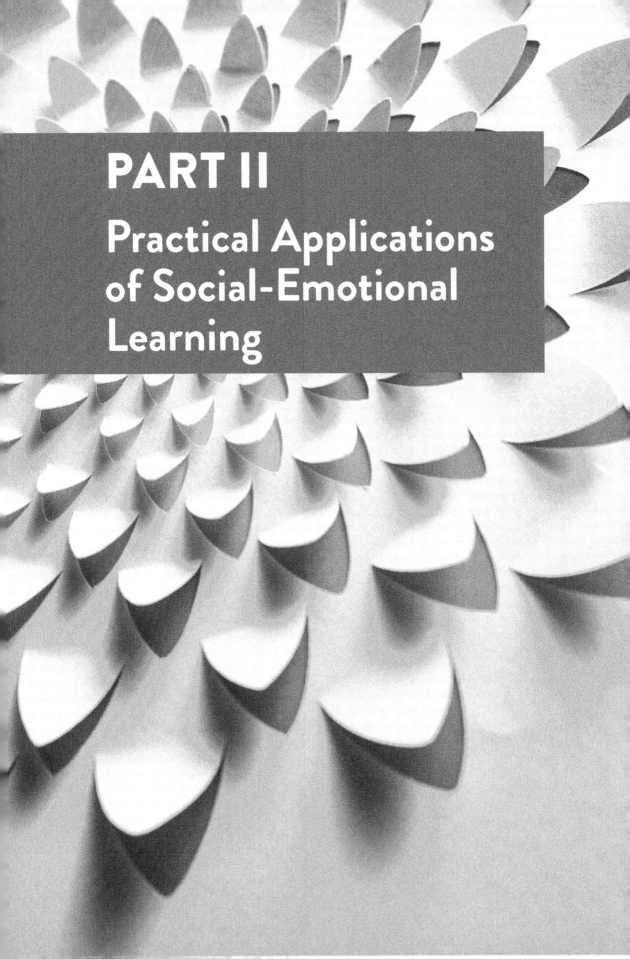

PART II
Practical Applications of Social-Emotional Learning

CHAPTER 4

Mindfulness

ZADIA'S STORY

Zadia works two jobs. She cleans during the week at a university, and she cleans on the weekend in an office building. While at the university one day, she asked one of the faculty members that she regularly talks to if she could get help filling out citizenship paperwork. The faculty member readily agreed and told her to bring it in. When the faculty member realized how long the form was, though, she told Zadia that they should set aside some time to work on it, in addition to their first meeting. Zadia was overwhelmed with the length of the required paperwork. She thought there were only a few pages out of the thick packet that needed to be completed.

The faculty member told her she was happy to help, but Zadia could not move forward with filling it out. She told the faculty member that she was going to think about whether she wanted to complete it. She came back a few weeks later and told the faculty member she was able to obtain the packet in Arabic, but that it made her realize that she wanted to learn English. She was going to start taking English classes in the evening. Yet, once she started, she was too tired to keep both of her jobs. Going from work, to school, to work again and again became a rut. She found herself sinking into depression because of the monotonous routine that had become her life.

We can easily get stuck in our routines, going through the motions to get through the day without stopping to be in the moment. Zadia could have benefited from using some time to be focused on herself in the present. Do you take time to be in the moment, with purpose, to help yourself to wake up from your day-to-day life? Mindfulness is accepting what we have, not taking our lives for granted, and not assuming things will always be the same. It is about being in the moment with openness and acceptance (Niemiec, 2017). You might have heard of mindfulness referred to as *mindfulness meditation.*

An example of mindfulness is focusing on your breathing or on images to help you relax. By doing this, you can relieve stress. Mindfulness can also help with anxiety, pain, depression, insomnia, and high blood pressure. Results can include better attention as well, as you take the time to pay attention to your environment, such as carefully savoring what you eat or enjoying nature while you walk outside. You should try to use mindfulness every day, even if it is just for a few minutes, to see how your outlook can change (Mayo Clinic Staff, 2020).

Using mindfulness in your English language classroom can also help everyone get into a positive mindset. It gives you time to work on yourself and teaches your students how to work on themselves, so everybody wins. In this chapter, we have three "Meet the Teacher" scenarios to demonstrate how some of your colleagues are using mindfulness. Let's start with Kristen from New York in the United States.

MEET THE TEACHER

Kristen Viig

English as a New/Second Language Teacher

Mill Road Intermediate School, Red Hook, New York, USA

I have been teaching English as a new/second language (ENL/ESL) for over 10 years. I love working with students from around the world and playing the role of ambassador for newcomers. My ENL/ESL classroom has always been a safe haven for English learners (ELs)—a stress-free place where we would sing songs, chant, play language games, and, most important, move as we practiced our language skills.

As EL populations increase across the United States, and public schools shift toward a more inclusive, integrated model for teaching ENL, it becomes increasingly important to bring mindfulness and social-emotional practices to the mainstream classroom. (ESL programs focus on English language acquisition, whereas ENL programs teach language arts and content area instruction using ENL instructional strategies.)

I would like to share some activities that my coteachers and I use to incorporate mindfulness and movement into our lessons. Stress ➜

is a language learning killer in many aspects. To reduce stress, I use the total physical response (TPR) method to allow my ELs to learn English using physical movement to react to verbal input. TPR creates a brain link between speech and action to boost language and vocabulary learning. Similar to the way babies learn their first language, this process reduces student inhibitions and lowers stress. You can also combine mindfulness and TPR with vocabulary instruction.

At our school, we have a theme of the month and a weekly precept that fits with that theme. I present this theme with its definition and an image as our focus for guided meditation.

Sample Meditation Script: Optimism

[Set the scene with calming sounds or music and turn down the lights. Students sit or stand with hands at their sides]. *Our theme is* optimism. [Read definition aloud.] *Every time you hear the word* optimism, *or picture something positive, lift your hands over your head and make a big sun and smile.* [Model this a few times before you begin.] *Now, clear your mind of all your outside thoughts. Be present, be here, in this moment. Let's focus on one thought. Optimism. Think about what optimism is to you. Think of a moment when you felt optimistic. As you close your eyes, picture yourself saying "I can do this, everything is going to be alright." As you breathe in, see your picture. As you breathe out, let yourself feel the optimism you are picturing and say silently to yourself, "I am optimistic." Feel yourself relax and feel optimism. Breathe in. Breathe out. "I am optimistic." Breathe in. "Good things will happen in the future."*

Optimism
a feeling or belief that good things will happen in the future. Optimism is looking on the bright side.

Yoga and meditation activities are also relaxing forms of TPR. Students follow verbal commands while learning vocabulary for body parts, prepositions, and verbs of motion in a relaxed and focused state of mind. Newcomers require more coaching, so it is helpful to clearly indicate which body part to use before the movement. I position myself near the newcomer so I can model and repeat any actions with more emphasis. I hope these activities will inspire you to incorporate movement and mindfulness into your daily routine, creating a stress-free, safe haven for all students—and smiles all around. ❖

Mindfulness Attitudes

There are seven mindfulness attitudes. As you read about them, think about how you are—or are not—using them. Keep an open mind about how you could use them in the future yourself and for your students.

1. **Nonjudging:** Be neutral with yourself and others.
2. **Patience:** Give yourself the time you need (without feeling guilty) to develop mindfulness.
3. **Beginner's mind:** Try to see things "for the first time."
4. **Trust:** Listen to what you think and believe; trust in yourself.
5. **Nonstriving:** Do not worry about working toward goals related to mindfulness; instead accept things as they are.
6. **Acceptance or acknowledgment:** Be present in the moment; accept things (even if you are not happy with them).
7. **Letting go/letting be:** If things are not going as planned or how you would like, practice letting it go or letting it be.

You might find nonstriving to be the hardest mindfulness attitude to adopt. It is for many of us because we tend to work toward goals, so not having goals can seem odd. However, by being nonstriving, you can remove any worries about mindfulness outcomes and further accept your current situation (Strauss, 2017). As you will see in the next "Meet the Teacher," Principal Brian Boyd is able to encourage his entire school to use mindfulness practices, giving his EL students the time needed to embrace mindfulness attitudes. Principal Boyd's words remind us that the successful incorporation of mindfulness and social-emotional learning (SEL) in our learning spaces is a community effort.

MEET THE TEACHER

Brian Boyd

Elementary School Principal

*Red Hook Central School District,
Red Hook, New York, USA*

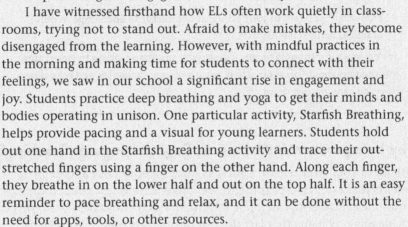

Working with our ELs is one of the most rewarding and soul-satisfying aspects of teaching and learning. Over the past several years, we have enhanced instruction at our school using mindfulness practices and activities to strengthen SEL. Supporting ELs with the use of mindfulness practices has helped strengthen engagement and resiliency.

I have witnessed firsthand how ELs often work quietly in classrooms, trying not to stand out. Afraid to make mistakes, they become disengaged from the learning. However, with mindful practices in the morning and making time for students to connect with their feelings, we saw in our school a significant rise in engagement and joy. Students practice deep breathing and yoga to get their minds and bodies operating in unison. One particular activity, Starfish Breathing, helps provide pacing and a visual for young learners. Students hold out one hand in the Starfish Breathing activity and trace their outstretched fingers using a finger on the other hand. Along each finger, they breathe in on the lower half and out on the top half. It is an easy reminder to pace breathing and relax, and it can be done without the need for apps, tools, or other resources.

When children struggle to learn a language or to read at grade level, they can develop anxiety about sharing out loud, but our students regularly share and talk about how they are feeling, and they are now advocating for themselves. One particular student from West Africa told us he needed to stand up more during the day to learn, so we rearranged the room and purchased a standing desk for him to work. He is now more engaged and focused on learning.

We want all students to feel comfortable and be ready to learn. Part of understanding how we learn best is to talk about our feelings and build greater self-awareness. Students often do not even realize that they have disconnected from a lesson or that they appear anxious or worried. It is exciting to see students share how they feel and be empowered to advocate for themselves.

What starts with just talking about feeling good or okay now looks like a classroom with all students able to express their feelings and look out for others. Mindfulness activities have brought all of our students closer together. In addition to advocating for themselves, ➜

expressing their feelings with classmates has also increased our ELs' confidence in reading. We have seen many more conversational skills being practiced, and improved speaking and listening, too! Taking the time to practice mindfulness activities with our students has provided a gateway to improved instruction and, more important, improved relationships with our students at our school. ❖

THINK BOX

The Starfish Breathing activity gives students a concrete way to help with their breathing.

- In what ways have you (or will you) helped your students breathe or engage in relaxation techniques?
- How might you talk to your principal or director to encourage mindful practices across classrooms?

Jot down your responses to these questions and keep reading to learn more information about this topic. Then, return to your responses and reflect on how you can improve them.

Why Incorporate Mindfulness in English Language Teaching?

With all of your requirements, such as meeting objectives and helping students pass assessments, it might seem like there is not enough time for mindfulness. However, just a few minutes in each class taken to do this can provide many benefits that last the rest of the class time. Here are a few easy and quick ways to incorporate mindfulness:

- Start each class with a pause to focus on something positive in students' lives while breathing in and out a few times.

- Insert mindfulness during class time as a break. Have students change their positions (stand, walk, move about) while taking a few moments to relax and pay attention to their breathing before continuing on to a new exercise.

- Think about how you can add some yoga or sports stretches, perhaps at the end of each class, to provide closure after you have summarized the lesson's objectives.

Mindfulness should not be thought of as another thing to do, rather something you and your students look forward to doing. This can be especially important for your ELs who are struggling to learn the language and/or are dealing with issues at home. In the next "Meet the Teacher," May F. Chung, an academic writing specialist, shares with us how she takes time with her students to include mindfulness.

MEET THE TEACHER

May F. Chung

Academic Writing Specialist

National Defense University, Washington DC, USA

As teachers of ESL are intimately aware, our students come from all walks of life. I am currently an academic writing specialist teaching adult international students at our institution. In my classes, I have had students who have witnessed genocide, discrimination, and violence in their home countries. When my students enter our classroom, they carry their own personal traumas with them. In these cases, mindfulness practices can help my students and me as we navigate these obstacles in the context of our classroom.

The first step of mindfulness practice is to set an intention. Consider that adult students may have many demands from work or from their home lives—and yet, they have made the choice to study a very difficult language! Be mindful of the ways in which students carry both internal and external pressures to learn a language. Ask the students to consider their goals around learning English. It is important here not to attach undesired feelings toward learning, such as the anguish of not being able to pronounce certain words or the frustration with not being able to have others understand you. Instead, have students reflect on how far they want to progress in their fluency. Do they want to communicate with their children? Would they like to advocate for themselves in public or without assistance? Do they want to dream in English?

The second step is to help students learn to appreciate their mistakes. Sometimes their language "errors" are actually a result of English's irregular usage and abundance of phrasal verbs. My own mother came to this country from Hong Kong over 30 years ago, and while she has a good grasp of English, she will make what I call "tiny mistakes." For example, instead of the word *expensive*, my mother will use the term *expense-ful*. Instead of correcting her on her English, I stop to evaluate and appreciate her words. In some ways, her way actually sounds better. This gave me a unique perspective so that when I am looking at a diamond, it seems "full of expense" rather than something that is inherently "expensive." When we are mindful and appreciative of our students using language in creative and meaningful ways, we are less likely to take these errors or mistakes as "failures" of our own teaching. ➔

Lastly, as teachers, we can be mindful of our students' learning trajectories and recognize how far they have come. It may be worthwhile to have students do a weekly writing exercise to explore how much English they have learned, or we can periodically share with our students their progress. An emphasis on mindfulness keeps things in balance so that students do not become so caught up in a task that they forget the steps they have walked in their language learning journey. While we cannot take away our students' painful past experiences, through the inclusion of mindful practices, we can help them be present in our learning spaces and share the current joy and compassion in a chaotic world. ✣

SEL in Action

In this section, we propose three lessons you can use to introduce mindfulness practices in your English language classroom. These lessons will focus on using idioms to promote optimism (Lesson 1), developing positive affirmations (Lesson 2), and using bird-related vocabulary to engage in breathing activities (Lesson 3). Keep in mind that these lessons should be modified and tailored to fit your students' ages, English levels, and individual needs. Also, depending on the length of your classes, these lessons may require more than one class period to complete.

Lesson 1: When Life Gives You Lemons, Make Lemonade

Language Objectives
Students will be able to engage all four primary language domains (listening, speaking, reading, and writing). They will listen to idioms that provide optimism, select one to write down, read aloud their selection to a peer, and narrate how they could use it in their lives.

Content Objectives
Students will be able to provide the definition of an idiom and will be able to identify idioms to promote optimism.

SEL Core Competencies
Self-awareness, self-management, social awareness, and relationship skills. In addition to aligning with the SEL core competencies, this lesson also aligns with Principle 1 ("know your learners"), Principle 2 ("create conditions for language learning"), Principle 3 ("design high-quality lessons for language development"), Principle 4 ("adapt lesson delivery as needed"), and Principle 5 ("monitor and assess student language development") from *The 6 Principles for Exemplary Teaching of English Learners®*.

Materials
Paper, drawing pencils, computer/phone/device with internet

Assessment

Formative or informal assessments for this lesson can be based on having students explain what specific idioms mean in real life, figuratively, and examples of how they can be demonstrated or exemplified (in writing and orally). The appropriateness of the idioms selected, along with their written explanations, can be used as a summative assessment.

Procedure

To get students interested in idioms, share some of your favorites to start, ensuring to select ones that portray optimism. For example, you could talk about the idiom "When life gives you lemons, make lemonade," explaining how it means always trying to see how something might be positive. Give examples, such as how you might prefer face-to-face instruction, but when your school requires online instruction, you realize it gives you the benefit of being able to wear comfortable pants and no shoes. In addition, you can have your puppy on your lap while you work. Of course, we can think about the negatives, but for this lesson, we will intentionally focus on the positives. Remember to adapt the example you provide to your students based on their language/age levels.

Provide a list of positive idioms, such as this one:

1. There are plenty of fish in the sea.
2. See the glass as half full instead of half empty.
3. When one door closes, another one opens.
4. Every cloud has a silver lining.
5. There is light at the end of the tunnel.
6. Stop and smell the roses.
7. See the world through rose-colored glasses.
8. That is a blessing in disguise.

Have students guess what these idioms might mean. Then, in small groups, have your students look up online the meaning of each idiom to verify if their guesses were correct. Let them either choose one of the idioms from your list (if their language proficiency would make it difficult to find one on their own) or look online for a different one that may be of more interest.

Next, have your students write down one idiom, illustrate it, and then write how they could use it in their lives. They can also do this in a word processing program or presentation software (e.g., Microsoft Word or PowerPoint, Google Docs or Slides) and find a visual online or take a picture, as shown in Figure 4.1. Check in with students using thumbs up/thumbs down to see if they are understanding and are following the directions. Once they are ready, they can share their work with a peer. In future classes, you can start class with one of the idioms, revisit the meaning, and practice breathing in and out while focusing on the positive as a soothing way to begin the day.

Figure 4.1 Positive idiom slide example.

Lesson 2: Positive Affirmations

Language Objectives
Students will be able to engage all four primary language domains (listening, speaking, reading, and writing). They will listen to positive affirmations starting with "I can" and will then write down two "I can" statements they want to work on. They will read and explain them to a partner and then make a banner for the wall (or add them to a class Padlet/Google Jamboard, etc.).

Content Objectives
Students will be able to provide the definition of a positive affirmation and will be able to develop positive affirmations related to the class objectives as well as their lives.

SEL Core Competencies
Self-awareness, self-management, and relationship skills. In addition to aligning with the SEL Core Competencies, this lesson also aligns with Principle 1 ("know your learners"), Principle 2 ("create conditions for language learning"), Principle 3 ("design high-quality lessons for language development"), Principle 4 ("adapt lesson delivery as needed"), and Principle 5 ("monitor and assess student language development") from *The 6 Principles for Exemplary Teaching of English Learners®*.

Materials
Poster paper, markers, computer/phone/device with internet

Assessment
Formative or informal assessments for this lesson can be based on students' interactions and discussions in small groups. For the summative assessment, collect students' written positive affirmation choices.

Procedure

If we think back, we might remember a teacher that did not let us say "I can't." Maybe it was your physical education teacher, for example? Maybe no matter how hard the task was, whether it was running around the field three times or doing as many sit-ups as you could in 1 minute, they always told you to say "I can."

Think of a time when you consciously told yourself, "I can," whether it was inspired by a teacher or not, and share some of those experiences with your students. Let them know how you had your doubts, but pushed through with "I can" statements. Share some examples of "I can" statements related to your class objectives and lives. What might be something you want students to accomplish? Maybe it is, "I can finish reading an entire story on my own." Perhaps it is, "I can help my peers during group time." After you give students examples, have them think of some on their own.

Have them write down two examples, one related to class and one related to their personal lives. Provide time for them to share within small groups, and then have them write the affirmations on poster paper (large strips) to post around the class. Alternatively, you could have them write the affirmations on sticky notes to post on the board. If you are online, you could have them write the affirmations into a Padlet (padlet.com), Google Jamboard (jamboard.google.com), or other similar program (see Figure 4.2). Check for comprehension to adjust the level of the task if necessary.

After the class has completed this activity, have them take time to reflect on their positive affirmations. Have them breathe in positivity and breathe out any negative thoughts related to their statements. Remind them to be in the moment and let go of anything that is bothering them. Remind them that taking this time to focus on their breathing will bring them energy. Have them breathe in and out slowly for at least a few

Positive Affirmations

I can...

I can think positive.

I can get my homework done.

I can eat healthier.

I can practice reading at home.

I can write in my journal every day.

I can start exercising.

I can study every day.

I can start doing yoga.

Figure 4.2 Examples of "I can" statements in Google Jamboard.

minutes. Ideally, you would have them breathing in and out for 10 or more minutes, but if you have class time constraints, a few minutes are better than none (Puddicombe, 2017). When you do this breathing activity, having soothing music in the background and relaxing scents might prove helpful.

Encourage your students to take time at home to focus on themselves by breathing in and out slowly, trying to breathe out longer than they breathe in. This will help them become relaxed and will help them feel less anxious or stressed, because it calms the nervous system (Berzin, 2020). It also helps them get ready to focus on studying, or on anything they want to learn to do (Mindworks Team, 2021). Then, during the next class, make sure to ask students how it went as a follow-up.

Lesson 3: Bird Breathing

Language Objectives
Students will be able to engage all four primary language domains (listening, speaking, reading, and writing). They will listen to and learn the names of five birds (or other animals of your choice) and ways to breathe based on the birds' size. They will select an animal based on their current emotional state, write down the animal's name, and provide an explanation about why they chose the animal and how they felt after breathing like the animal. Last, they will read their explanation to a partner.

Content Objectives
Students will be able to analyze and explain their animal selections based on the way they are feeling and describe how they feel after the breathing exercise.

SEL Core Competencies
Self-awareness, self-management, social awareness, relationship skills, and responsible decision-making. In addition to aligning with the SEL Core Competencies, this lesson also aligns with Principle 1 ("know your learners"), Principle 2 ("create conditions for language learning"), Principle 3 ("design high-quality lessons for language development"), Principle 4 ("adapt lesson delivery as needed"), and Principle 5 ("monitor and assess student language development") from *The 6 Principles for Exemplary Teaching of English Learners*®.

Materials
Paper, pen, dry erase board, dry erase marker, computer/phone/device with internet

Assessment
Formative or informal assessments for this lesson can be based on observations of students' engagement during the whole group activity and while in pairs. The summative assessment is based on students' writing exercise.

Procedure

Start by asking students to tell you how they feel with a quick show on their fingers. Use a scale from 1 to 5, with 1 being very calm and 5 being very anxious or upset. Next, show them visuals for five birds (or any animals you think they can benefit from learning the names of and order them from small to large). This activity will be more meaningful if you include birds or animals living in your community or surroundings that students see regularly. For example, the following birds can be found in Maryland, USA:

1. Sparrow
2. Bluebird
3. Oriole
4. Raven
5. Eagle

Explain that they should envision that, as each animal on the list gets bigger than the previous one, it has larger lungs requiring more air to breathe. If the student is feeling calm, they should consider sparrow breaths, where they breathe in for a four-count (1-2-3-4) and out for a four-count (1-2-3-4), called equal breathing (Gotter, 2019). However, the more anxious or upset they feel, the larger the bird they should choose, and the deeper their breath would be, with exhales longer than inhales and focus on their breathing: how their body feels as they breathe, including their nose, lungs, and the cool air coming through them. (Adapt your breathing explanation based on your students' language/age levels.)

After breathing in and out based on their bird of choice for a few minutes, have them write down how the focused breathing made them feel. In addition, have them explain why they selected that bird and how they went about breathing in and out as a result. They can also draw the bird selected next to their explanation. Check for understanding after providing directions by having them write "yes" for *I understand* or "no" for *I do not understand* on a response board/dry erase board.

Once they have completed their journal entry, have them share with a peer. They can try breathing using their peer's animal selection, or, if their peer made the same animal selection, they can use the same animal again or try a different one for additional breathing practice.

The next time you try bird breathing with your students, go outside (if possible) to look for birds. After viewing a few different size birds and helping students name the birds, practice bird breathing while focusing on nature and the fresh air. Being outside and having the opportunity to change environments will help everyone reset their moods. You can also have a conversation about the similarities and differences between the birds students see in the neighborhood and the birds they have in their native countries.

ADDITIONAL RESOURCE

For more information to continue the discussion about birds with students, see the following:

Active Wild. (2018). *Birds: The ultimate guide. Amazing bird facts, pictures, and information.* www.activewild.com/birds

In Summary

This chapter provides many ideas to think about and use in your English language classroom to introduce mindfulness to your ELs. We discussed the following:

1. The definition of mindfulness
2. Mindfulness attitudes
3. Reasons to incorporate mindfulness in English language teaching
4. Idioms that provide optimism (Lesson 1)
5. Positive affirmations (Lesson 2)
6. Bird breathing (Lesson 3)

The activities shared throughout this chapter can be used for any grade or language proficiency level with accommodations based on student needs. We hope you find these ideas useful for your classrooms tomorrow. Let's continue the dialogue online—there is still much more to explore. We can all learn from each other. Look for our conversation on social media using #SELforELs.

CHAPTER 5

Peace Education

"Language actively shapes and gives meaning to human experience."
—A. L. Wenden (1995, p. 216)

ANTIKOT'S STORY

As soon as the bell rings, students come rushing inside the classroom to begin their first class for the day—English for Newcomers. Before the English language teacher, Mrs. Rasmus, begins to take attendance, she checks in with everyone: "Good morning class, how are you feeling today?" Most students respond to her question almost in unison, but Mrs. Rasmus notices that Antikot, a student who is always smiling and full of energy, seems unsettled.

Mrs. Rasmus takes attendance and while the rest of the class is working on a warm-up activity on the board, she discreetly asks Antikot to accompany her outside of the class. "Are you okay, Antikot? You look sad," Mrs. Rasmus asks. Antikot shares with Mrs. Rasmus that during breakfast, in the school cafeteria, she did not see a girl (another student); she bumped into her by mistake and said, "Excuse me." The girl turned around and began yelling at Antikot, saying, "You are not excused!" Antikot did not understand why the other student was so upset when she apologized after bumping into her.

Antikot's vignette is a real story that happens to many English learners (ELs) who are still learning the pragmatic effects of the words and phrases we use in the English language. In Antikot's particular case, she used the expression *excuse me* to apologize after bumping by mistake into the other student. In English, we usually use the phrase *excuse me* to ask someone to politely move or to call someone's attention. The correct phrase Antikot should have used to apologize after doing something wrong or hurting someone is *I am sorry*. In this exchange, it seems that the other student misunderstood by Antikot's *excuse me* that Antikot was asking her to move out of the way after bumping into her, which resulted in the other student feeling upset and yelling. Minor pragmatic misunderstandings, such as the one displayed in Antikot's vignette, occur every day to ELs and even among native speakers, causing tension and conflict. Through the infusion of peace education, ELs can learn techniques and vocabulary they can use to de-escalate uncomfortable situations that may lead to violence.

What Is Peace?

In most cultures, peace is understood as a state of tranquility, quiet, or harmony in personal relations. In a social and global sense, peace is often associated with happiness, prosperity, respect, friendship, and agreements. The absence of peace results in conflicts, such as violence and war, and it can also lead to undesired feelings (e.g., fear, depression) when we cannot find peace within ourselves. Peace and conflict are directly connected to one another: Peace is achieved through the de-escalation of and effective response to conflict; conflict thrives in an atmosphere of disrespect, unhappiness, and inflexibility. Figure 5.1 shows a brief overview of the interconnection between conflict and peace as well as some of the steps that individuals can take to attain balance or to gravitate toward either side of the spectrum.

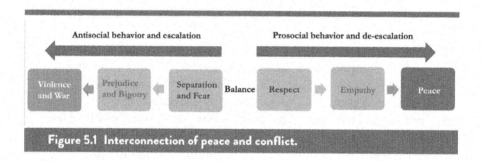

Figure 5.1 Interconnection of peace and conflict.

What Is Peace Education?

Peace education is generally defined as both a philosophy and a process prioritizing the acquisition of knowledge, skills, attitudes, behaviors, and values for the conservation of peace through conflict resolutions (Bajaj, 2008; Harris & Morrison, 2013). Within the interdisciplinary field of peace studies, peace education is involved with teaching students how to maintain social and global peace through nonviolence, de-escalation, and conflict resolution techniques. Peace education is also committed to cultivating values that promote societal cooperation, awareness of our planet, and global citizenship.

Social-Emotional Learning in the English Language Classroom

Today, peace education initiatives can be found at various institutions, each focusing on general or specific topics at different levels (e.g., global peace, societal peace, or peace in the community). For the purpose of this chapter and book, we understand *peace education* as the philosophy and practices educators of ELs use to cultivate the skills needed to successfully resolve conflict and preserve peace.

THINK BOX

According to Indian scriptures, there are three kinds of violence: mental (*manasik*), verbal (*vachik*), and physical (*kayeek*).

- **Mental:** Thinking of hurting others, regardless of whether physical harm is actually done. Thoughts like "I wish I had hit that person hard" are mental violence. Thinking ill of others is also a form of violence.

- **Verbal:** Use of harsh words is another form of violence. Words have the power to hurt or heal people.

- **Physical:** Using physical force to harm others is the most commonly recognized form of violence between individuals, groups, communities, and countries.

(UNESCO, 2005)

How do you plan to explore these three forms of violence with your students? What type of activities can you incorporate to teach your ELs some techniques to avoid violence at these three levels (mental, verbal, and physical) and preserve peace?

Jot down your responses to these questions and keep reading to learn more information about this topic. Then, return to your responses and reflect on how you can improve them.

Why Incorporate Peace Education in English Language Teaching?

Language—both verbal and nonverbal—has a role in creating misunderstandings, de-escalating conflicts, and attaining and preserving peace. This is an important statement that we need to keep in mind when we are teaching English to our ELs because not having (or knowing) the appropriate vocabulary can lead to miscommunication and conflict, as we saw demonstrated at the beginning of this chapter in Antikot's story. At the same time, we have to keep in mind that nonverbal language (e.g., body movement and posture, gestures, personal space, physical touch, facial expressions, and eye contact, to name a few) can also lead to misunderstandings and conflict. When ELs arrive in our classrooms, they are taught to listen, read, write, and speak in English. However, they also need to learn how to use appropriate forms of nonverbal language in the new host country, which may greatly differ from the nonverbal language they were taught and exposed to in their native cultures. Through peace education, educators can teach ELs the appropriate verbal and nonverbal language they need to de-escalate conflict and violence arising from miscommunication.

Peace education is usually not a topic addressed in teachers of English to speakers of other languages (TESOL) preparation programs, but it does influence the communication, interaction, and success of our ELs as students and in their lives beyond formal education. Communication has the power to preserve peace or, in cases of miscommunications, disrupt it. For example, in some cultures, calling someone "fat" is a compliment denoting prosperity and beauty. However, if our ELs try to compliment an American-born classmate by calling them "fat," this communication will create a conflict that could result in the disruption of peace or even escalate to violence. The same occurs with nonverbal communication; for example, in the United States, entering someone's personal space is considered rude and intrusive. For some of our ELs, however, being in close physical proximity to someone or even touching that person while talking to them is considered a sign of appreciation.

MEET THE TEACHER

Manuel De Jesús Gómez Portillo

Middle School English to Speakers of Other Languages Resource Teacher

Fairfax County Public Schools, Fairfax, Virginia, USA

Having a sense of community in school is important for the mental health and academic achievement of students. A sense of community provides students with safety, comfort, focus, and inner peace. The school where I work is one of the most diverse in the Commonwealth of Virginia. Although over 90% of the students are identified as language minority students, not all are categorized as ELs. In fact, only about 30% of the students in my school are classified as ELs. This diversity in our student population sometimes creates a truly interesting school environment where ELs and non-ELs have misunderstandings, leading to conflicts and unstable relationships between the two groups.

One day, my ELs and I were taking a break from an English language development lesson when I heard two of my eighth graders talking. One student said, "¿Por qué creen que son mejores que nosotros? [Why do they think they are better than us?]" ➜

The other student replied, "*No entiendo, somos del mismo país y se burlan de nosotros porque estamos aprendiendo inglés* [I don't understand, we are from the same country and they make fun of us because we are learning English]."

Curious to learn more about what my students were talking about, I set up time during lunch to meet with both of them. Once we took the time to talk, my students explained that some of their non-EL classmates were making fun of them for being ELs and immigrants. The students explained that this was making them feel uncomfortable and that they were developing feelings of not wanting to come to school. In order to make the school environment better for my students and their non-EL counterparts, I decided to hold weekly meetings during lunchtime where I would invite ELs and non-ELs to eat together.

Each lunch session usually begins with students walking in the classroom with their food and finding a seat to eat. I always make sure to sit next to different students, and I also ensure that students are sitting next to different classmates each time we meet. This allows us to get to know each other better and to build relationships. During each 30-minute lunch meeting, we talk about our interests (music, sports, etc.) and about school life. For instance, during one lunch meeting, we talked about our favorite soccer teams. Then, we talked about other issues, such as the experiences of EL and non-EL students at our school. What I have noticed is that these lunch meetings have built bridges between the two groups. In fact, most of them have become friends outside of school and pursue common hobbies together, such as playing soccer. I have also noticed that after implementing lunch meetings, my ELs have been more attentive during class, and their grades have started to get better. I followed up with the two students I described in the opening paragraph, and they told me that they feel more welcomed at school and that they feel a sense of community.

Sometimes, misunderstandings between students in school can lead to stress, fear, and a sense of inferiority. Providing a space for ELs and non-ELs to meet, share, and reflect upon their hobbies, interests, and experiences allows them to build relationships, work interpersonal peace, and increase their capacities to proactively address conflicts. Furthermore, by building a sense of community in school, their social-emotional needs can be addressed. Last, taking the time to learn about and address issues impacting the lives of ELs can provide a school climate where respect, empathy, and peace are practiced. Often, it can be as simple as providing students with an informal setting, such as meeting during lunch to share and reflect and partake in proactive actions that lead to the preservation of inner peace and peace in our schools. ❖

The concept of peace applies to almost every context (e.g., political, social, global). However, for the purpose of this chapter and book, we are interested in fostering the cultivation of peace in three main contexts:

- Inner Peace: Inner peace means finding harmony, calm, and contentedness within ourselves. To achieve inner peace, we must learn to understand our feelings and how to de-escalate inner conflicts when necessary.

- Interpersonal Peace: Social relationships focus on daily interactions with people in our life, such as with family, coworkers, classmates, and neighbors. Interpersonal peace is about sustaining harmonious, respectful, and cooperative relationships with those people, avoiding harm, conflict, and violence. Engaging in interpersonal peace is, in its simplest form, learning how to live together, which is helpful for maintaining positive social environments.

- Ecological Peace: Ecological peace involves reconnecting with nature through the adoption of practices at different levels that protect the natural environment, animals, and the Earth.

(Oxford et al., 2021)

In what ways do you engage your ELs in cultivating peace in these three contexts? What practices do you include or can include in your learning environment to teach your students about cultivating inner, interpersonal, and ecological peace?

Jot down your responses to these questions and keep reading to learn more information about this topic. Then, return to your responses and reflect on how you can improve them.

SEL in Action

In this section, we propose three lessons you can use to introduce peace education in your English language classroom. These lessons focus on fostering inner, interpersonal, and ecological peace (Oxford et al., 2021). For the best results, these three lessons should be implemented in the order they are presented because they introduce the concept of peace (Lesson 1), give students the opportunity to dismantle misconceptions of peace and conflict (Lesson 2), and explore tips you can use to promote and achieve inner peace and connect with nature (Lesson 3).

Keep in mind that these lessons should be modified and tailored to fit your students' ages, English levels, and individual needs. Also, depending on the length of your classes, these lessons may require more than one class period to complete.

Lesson 1: Introducing Peace

Language Objectives

Students will be able to engage all four primary language domains (listening, speaking, reading, and writing) to describe their definition of peace, gain knowledge about their classmates' definitions of peace, and collaboratively produce a poster describing the classroom's communal definition of peace.

Content Objectives

Students will be able to compare and contrast different points of view related to the definition of peace and build consensus on a definition of peace for the classroom.

SEL Core Competencies

Self-awareness, social awareness, and relationship skills. In addition to aligning with the SEL core competencies, this lesson also aligns with Principle 1 ("know your learners"), Principle 2 ("create conditions for language learning"), and Principle 3 ("design high-quality lessons for language development") from *The 6 Principles for Exemplary Teaching of English Learners*®.

Materials

Introducing the word *peace* activity (Table 5.1), materials for poster or access to computer/phone/device with internet.

Assessment

Formative or informal assessments can be conducted continuously by evaluating students' participation in class and group discussions. The activities shared in Table 5.1 (worksheet) and the peace poster students create can be used as summative assessments.

Procedure

The first step to instituting peace education is to introduce and explore the different understandings of the concept of *peace*. English language classrooms are rich, heterogenous learning spaces with ELs who have unique views on peace and on how to achieve and maintain it. At times, these diverse perspectives on peace may result in friction or tension. For this reason, introducing peace and achieving a general consensus of how it will be defined in the classroom is essential.

To introduce the word *peace*, simply write it on the board, read it aloud, and then ask students to join you in a class read-aloud. After you have read it in unison, ask "What is peace?" and invite students to share their views. Take notes somewhere visible (e.g., side of the board, or easel pad) for the whole class to see as they share their responses aloud. Then, without agreeing or disagreeing with students' responses at this point, divide the class in small groups so students can discuss the meaning further.

After 5–10 minutes of small-group discussion, share Table 5.1 and ask students to complete it individually. Depending on the English level of your students, the prompts in Table 5.1 can be modified to reflect the content you are teaching. For example, if you are teaching newcomers early in the year, you may provide translation in the students' native languages and allow them to write their responses in their native languages and then translate them into English. Conversely, if you are teaching intermediate or advanced students, you may choose to ask for descriptive vocabulary involving all five senses to describe peace.

Table 5.1 Introducing the Word *Peace*				
		Peace		
The word for *peace* in my native language is . . .	Peace feels like . . .	Peace looks like . . . (make a drawing!)	A peaceful memory I have is . . .	My definition of peace is . . .

After students complete the activity in Table 5.1, ask them to return to their small groups and have them share with their classmates. Depending on your class size, you may be inclined to share students' responses through a whole-class conversation. At this juncture, have students identify common key points they see throughout their responses, write them down somewhere visible in the classroom, and guide them toward a communal definition of peace by using those common key points.

As you explore the definition of peace, you may also wish to share with students the example poster in Figure 5.2 and explain the relationship between conflict and peace. Then, as a class, create a poster, either in the classroom or virtually using free graphic design platforms, such as Canva (www.canva.com). During the creation of this poster, all students will have the opportunity to contribute to the communal definition of peace that will be used in the classroom, include visual representations (e.g., drawings of olive branches, the peace sign), and write the translation of the word *peace* in their native languages. This poster will become a visual point of reference students can use for the duration of the school year to remember how peace is understood and respected in their English language classroom.

Lesson 2: Dismantling Misconceptions of Peace and Conflict

Language Objectives

Students will be able to engage all four primary language domains (listening, speaking, reading, and writing) to dismantle misconceptions of peace and conflict through conversations, active listening, reading of famous quotes, and responding in writing to a conflict exercise.

Content Objectives

Students will be able to state fundamental misconceptions of *peace* and *conflict*, identify techniques and behaviors for conflict de-escalation, and draw direct conclusions about the consequences of their actions.

SEL Core Competencies

Self-awareness, self-management, social awareness, relationship skills, and responsible decision-making. In addition to aligning with the SEL core competencies, this lesson also aligns with Principle 1 ("know your learners"), Principle 2 ("create conditions for language learning"), and Principle 3 ("design high-quality lessons for language development") from *The 6 Principles for Exemplary Teaching of English Learners*®.

Materials

Video, pictures, or reading activities of famous pacifists and peacemakers; common automatic responses to conflict (Figure 5.3); and "Responding to Conflict" exercise (Appendix A).

Assessment

Formative or informal assessments can be conducted continuously by evaluating students' participation in class and group discussions. The activity shared in Appendix A can be used as a summative assessment.

Procedure

One of the many benefits associated with incorporating peace education into teaching is that it gives students the opportunity to engage in deep critical thinking and metacognition (Harris & Morrison, 2013; Oxford, 2013). As educators promoting peace, we must keep in mind that giving our students the opportunity to explore their understanding of both *peace* and *conflict* is essential to dismantling misconceptions. For example, in our own professional practice we have learned that young learners—and some adult learners, too!—sometimes understand that responding to conflict with nonviolence is seen as a sign of cowardice. For example, if someone is hit and chooses to resolve this conflict by speaking, they might be perceived as being a coward because they did not respond with another hit. Similarly, our students would sometimes associate escalation or confrontation of conflict with strength and valor. For example, if a student is hit and chooses to hit back, they would be considered strong and brave. Lesson 2 is a lesson divided into two activities where we propose strategies you can use to dismantle these and other misconceptions associated with *peace* and *conflict*.

Activity 1: Dismantling Misconceptions of Peace

The purpose of Activity 1 is three-fold:

- to introduce students to peace vocabulary, such as *pacifist* and *peacemaker*,
- to learn about peacemakers and pacifists and their achievements, and
- to dismantle any misconceptions of peace.

To begin this activity, introduce peace vocabulary, such as the words *peacemaker* and *pacifist*. The introduction, depending on the level of your English class, can be a simple definition, such as:

- Pacifists are people who avoid violence and love peace.
- Peacemakers are people who take actions to restore peace by ending conflict.

When you introduce this peace vocabulary, you may choose to associate the words with important historical figures. For example, one of the most well-known pacifists is Mohandas Karamchand Gandhi, commonly known as "Mahatma" Gandhi; another well-known peacemaker is Susan Brownell Anthony. While introducing these historical figures, you may choose to share a picture, a short video, well-known quotes, or important details of their achievements. Depending on your preference and students' English levels, this activity has the potential to become a culminating class project where students are tasked with researching and presenting information about historical figures who were either pacifists or peacemakers.

After introducing the peace vocabulary and historical figures, create opportunities where students can reflect on their misconceptions of peace. For example, you may state or write on the board:

> "Engaging in peace means avoiding and de-escalating conflict. What do you think, for example, about a student who is hit by another student and chooses to talk instead of hitting back?"

Another option could be sharing with students a peace-related quote from an important historical figure, such as Cesar Chavez:

> "Non-violence is not inaction. It is not discussion. It is not for the timid or weak . . . Non-violence is hard work. It is the willingness to sacrifice. It is the patience to win." (United Farm Workers, n.d.)

Ask them to reflect on the quote, asking prompting questions as needed.

The goal of this part of the activity is for students to reflect about their perspective on conflict resolution and perceptions about individuals who choose to avoid violence or conflict. Keep in mind that the diversity of cultures and life experiences in your English language classroom will probably be reflected in your students' responses. You may see, for example, how some cultures value peace over violence, while other cultures may require boys and men to respond to conflict with conflict (i.e., physical confrontation with physical confrontation) to preserve their masculinity. At this juncture, be prepared to acknowledge and respect your students' diverse views. Also, share with them the preferred cultural practices (and consequences of engaging or not engaging in those practices) treasured in their new host society. Have prepared activities (e.g., role-plays, acting, drills) where they can learn these practices through rehearsal and repetition.

Activity 2: Dismantling Misconceptions of Conflict

Once students explore their views on peace and on how other people respond to conflict (Activity 1), they will be ready to learn about how *they* respond to conflict. How students respond to conflict will determine what steps they need to take to foster peace at the inner, social, and ecological levels. In Activity 2, keep in mind that peace exists by successfully coping with conflict, and that the mitigation and de-escalation of conflict fosters nonviolence, which leads to peace.

To begin Activity 2, ask students what the word *conflict* means to them. Please allow ELs to look for a translation if needed and provide examples or short stories that illustrate what conflict looks like. After listening to a few students, you may notice that for many, the word *conflict* carries a negative connotation and it is often associated with anger, violence, or war.

At this juncture, it is important to expand our students' understanding of the word *conflict* and explain that conflict itself is not a problem, but a natural part of life. Let students know that conflict (both internal and external) gives us opportunities to learn about ourselves and others, and grow. Also, explain to students that when they are confronted with conflict, there are many possible ways to react to it, and the way they react and handle conflict will influence the preservation or absence of peace (i.e., our response to conflict has consequences). Figure 5.3 demonstrates a visual of common automatic responses people have when confronted with conflict. It is important for students to see and understand that there are multiple ways, including nonviolent ways, of responding to conflict.

At this point, ask students how they act in uncomfortable situations. Depending on the English level of your class, you might phrase the question as "What do you do in uncomfortable situations?" or "What is your first reaction to conflict?" Some students might respond by saying that they prefer to laugh, make jokes, or simply run away. Other students might share their inclination to confront or fight the conflict or person creating the conflict, which may include fighting themselves in the case of inner conflicts. After listening to students' responses, write the statement "Your response to conflict affects peace" on the board and ask students if they agree or disagree with this statement, and then have them elaborate on their response. Alternatively, ask students to write their responses instead of engaging in a class discussion.

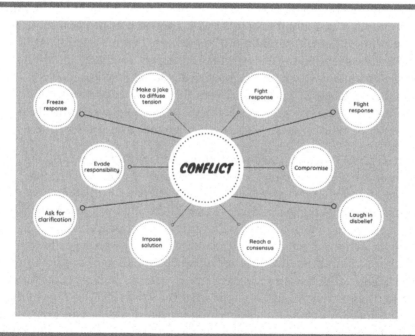

Figure 5.3 Common human automatic responses to conflict.

After students have the opportunity to reflect and share their experiences of how they respond to conflict, transition into the last portion of the exercise—the "Responding to Conflict" exercise (Appendix A). An effective way to introduce the exercise is to follow the *I do, we do, you do* format, where you model the activity in front of your students (I do), then work with your class to respond to an activity or task together (we do), and then you divide the class into small groups so they can work in groups or individually (you do).

For this activity, share with students a conflict/problem, a relationship graphic of your choice, and a space for essay-writing where students reflect on how their responses to conflict may produce different outcomes (see Appendix A for an example). An alternative to this exercise is sharing conflict scenarios with students and discussing as a class or in small groups effective ways to respond to these conflicts (both internal and external conflicts) and the outcomes those responses could produce.

Lesson 3: Promoting and Achieving Inner Peace

Language Objectives
Students will be able to apply active listening skills to practice techniques that promote inner peace.

Content Objectives
Students will be able to integrate techniques and practices they find helpful to de-escalate and manage inner conflict and achieve inner peace.

SEL Core Competencies
Self-awareness, self-management, and responsible decision-making. In addition to aligning with the SEL core competencies, this lesson also aligns with Principle 1 ("know your learners"), Principle 2 ("create conditions for language learning"), and Principle 3 ("design high-quality lessons for language development") from *The 6 Principles for Exemplary Teaching of English Learners*®.

Materials
Any toy or material where students can see what balance and imbalance looks like, and a computer/phone/device with internet or access to relaxing music.

Assessment
Formative or informal assessments for this lesson can be based on students' daily engagement in this activity. A summative assessment can be asking students to keep a journal where they record how they are engaging in activities inside and outside of school that contribute to their inner peace. Depending on your teaching context, you can assign monthly, quarterly, or yearly grades to this journaling activity.

Procedure
This lesson focuses on engaging in activities and daily practices that promote inner peace. To do this, it is important that we—and our students—

understand what inner peace is. Although different definitions exist, inner peace or peace of mind is thought of as a mental state of tranquility and calm. Inner peace is not achieved by eliminating outside stressors but, rather, by calming conflicts and turmoil that exists within ourselves. For this reason, to achieve inner peace, we must engage in daily practices that give us the opportunity to quiet down inner voices aggravating undesired feelings and emotions. The absence of inner peace leads, in many cases, to unhappiness and agitation, which may in turn lead to interpersonal conflict and violence. The end goal of this activity is for students to understand that if we allow daily stressors around us to disrupt us, it could create inner conflicts that could result in undesired feelings and interpersonal conflicts.

To introduce the concept of inner peace to your students, show students a balance toy or object. For our example, we will use a wooden balance board (Figure 5.4) to introduce students to inner peace. In class, use the balance board in front of your students. You may initially wobble on the balance board, but eventually you will reach balance. Once balance has been reached, connect the concept of balance to your students' lives. Depending on the level of your class, this statement may be something like, "This is balance. In our lives, sometimes we wobble because we have many problems, but we have to learn to balance ourselves or we will fall from the balance board." This may also be a good opportunity to teach vocabulary like *wobble* and *balance* and make real-life connections. An easy example for a newcomer's class could look like this:

- Wobble: Move from side to side
- Balance: Harmony and stability

We are using total physical response to connect *wobble* to problems and situations we deal with on a daily basis and to connect *balance* to inner peace.

Now that students understand the concept of achieving balance, we need to teach them how they can do this in their lives. You can tell students that "to achieve balance, we need to practice daily activities that help us feel peace inside of us." Create an opportunity where students can respond to the question, "What activities do you do every day to feel relaxed and at peace?" Students may respond to this question individually in their notebooks or orally in small groups. Some possible answers that students may share include talking with someone they care about, writing and reading (e.g., poetry, songs, journal), exercising, creating art, or other activities, like playing with their pets, playing games, or sitting down by themselves. Once students have shared with their peers, let them know that you will teach them a 5- to 10-minute strategy they can use every day to promote and achieve inner peace. If the learning environment permits, you may include this daily strategy in your classroom during the first 5–10 minutes of class to reinforce the practice and allow students to calm the energy they may bring from the outside world.

For this activity, you need a free product or app where you can play relaxation music, such as Calm (www.calm.com), Spotify (www.spotify.com),

or YouTube (www.youtube.com). Tell students that you will play relaxation music for 5–10 minutes, and they will meditate by focusing on their breathing. Different from mindfulness (Chapter 4), where the goal is to raise individual awareness of *something*, the purpose of meditation is to help students clear their minds and think of *nothing*. While playing relaxing music, you may choose to also do a guided meditation, which may require you to preteach vocabulary to your ELs, for example: "Close your eyes, relax your shoulders, breathe in and breath out." A variation of this activity you can also do is take students outside and allow them to walk around nature for 5–10 minutes while listening to relaxing music with their headphones or just have them sit down next to a tree and meditate.

Students might be a little confused when you initially introduce this practice in your learning space because they may not understand how engaging in activities that promote and teach inner peace are relevant in a formal school environment. They may find it helpful when you explain to them the importance of developing and engaging in inner peace now in school, but also in their future as adults. Also, you may share with students that life is full of obstacles and situations where they will find themselves wobbling (connecting to the activity of the curvy balance board). However, by engaging in practices that cultivate inner peace every day, even if just for a few minutes, they will feel more balanced, and the possibilities for inner conflicts will be reduced. Inner peace, in turn, will also contribute to reducing interpersonal conflict because when people are calm and have achieved peace of mind, they are less irritable and more patient and understanding with others. You will find that with consistency and guidance, students will begin to appreciate this daily activity of inner peace as they witness the calming results it produces through the remainder of your class.

Note that some free products, such as the Headspace (www.headspace .com) and Stop, Breathe, and Think (www.stopbreathethink.com) apps, provide additional features to promote inner peace and calm, including guided meditation, sleep stories, and breathing exercises. You may want to explore these free apps for yourself first, to then share with your students to help them achieve inner peace outside of school.

MEET THE TEACHER

Paulina Kurevija

Elementary English Language Development Teacher

Waterloo Region District School Board, Waterloo, Ontario, Canada

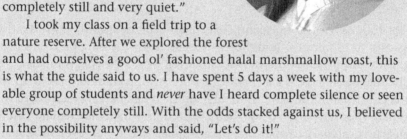

"For the chickadees to come eat from our hands we will have to be completely still and very quiet."

I took my class on a field trip to a nature reserve. After we explored the forest and had ourselves a good ol' fashioned halal marshmallow roast, this is what the guide said to us. I have spent 5 days a week with my loveable group of students and *never* have I heard complete silence or seen everyone completely still. With the odds stacked against us, I believed in the possibility anyways and said, "Let's do it!"

As we formed a line on the wooden bridge above a frozen marsh, my students stood with their excitement bubbling out. I stood at the end of the line, looking at each of my students trying their hardest to stand "as still as a statue." Then . . . I saw one of my students start to wiggle and fidget (as is her nature). And then, more and more students started to move. After about 30 seconds, a student of mine said very loudly, "No birds are coming!"

I gently said, "Shhh, they won't come if they hear us talking," to which he responded, "Why do you always get ME in trouble?!" Immediately, another student in my class yelled down the line, "STOP TALKING!," and, just like that, the chaos.

These memories are so fond in my mind. I never ask for the chaos to stop; we just slowly learn day by day to build a little more peace. That day, we built peace because we made it to 30 seconds with everyone as focused as they could be. We ran, explored, and tested out how many kids it would take to wrap their arms around the biggest tree in the forest; we connected with nature.

I teach in a specialized English Language Development program where most of my students and their families have come to Canada as refugees. Some of my students have seen violence, others were directly impacted by the violence. Many have never had the opportunity to attend school or were made to clean the schools instead of learning in them. Many of my amazing, resilient students grew ➔

up in a world of chaos, and when you are surrounded by chaos, eventually the chaos seeps in. Through nature we focus on building peace day by day. Field trips are exciting, but you do not need heavily wooded forests; even an open field with a few trees will do. Here are a few things we practice:

Explorers in Nature. We first make a list of the things we hope to find on our walks. It could be bugs, colorful leaves, a bird's nest. Students each have a small notebook to record their observations, and then we head out for a walk as explorers and scientists. (Tools like binoculars and magnifying glasses make this even more fun!) Sometimes we write our discoveries, and other times we draw them, letting art focus our attention on the details.

5-4-3-2-1 in Nature. We practice the mindfulness strategy "5-4-3-2-1 in nature." We all sit on the grass (or stand in the snow) and I prompt our class for each number as they share out loud:

5 things you see
4 things you hear
3 things you feel
2 things you smell
1 thing you are thankful for

Races in Nature. Trauma and stress manifest themselves in physical ways in the body. My students often say they have stomach aches, sore muscles, sore backs, or headaches. While there is a time and place for quiet peace, there is also a necessity for *fun* peace. The kind of peace that comes after running your fastest and laughing your hardest. I love to do races outside. ("First you have to touch the tree to the right, then one lap around the baseball diamond before touching the building, and then run back here!") Multistep challenges keep students focused, as running and laughing help the body process and let go of some of the trauma. A bit of nature can make a big impact. ❖

In Summary

This chapter provides three lessons you can use in your classroom to introduce peace education to your ELs. We discussed the following:

1. A brief overview of peace and peace education

2. The need for including peace education in English language teaching

3. How to introduce peace in the English language classroom (Lesson 1)

4. Ways to dismantle misconceptions of peace and conflict (Lesson 2)

5. Opportunities to engage in inner peace by meditating and walking in nature (Lesson 3)

ADDITIONAL RESOURCES

For additional resources you may find helpful and relevant to incorporating peace education in your English language class, see the following:

- Peace Worksheets and Resources (Reflection Press): reflectionpress.com/free-stuff/see-peace-worksheets-resources
- Teacher's Guide to Peace Education (UNESCO): unesdoc.unesco.org/ark:/48223/pf0000125228
- Peace Education E-Journal (U.S. Department of State): americanenglish.state.gov/resources/language-and-civil-society-e-journal-peace-education
- Peace Teachers Program (U.S. Institute for Peace): www.usip.org/public-education/educators/peace-teachers-program

The activities shared throughout this chapter can be used for any grade or language proficiency level with accommodations based on student needs. We hope you find these ideas useful for your classrooms tomorrow. Let's continue the dialogue online—there is still much more to explore. We can all learn from each other. Look for our conversation on social media using #SELforELs.

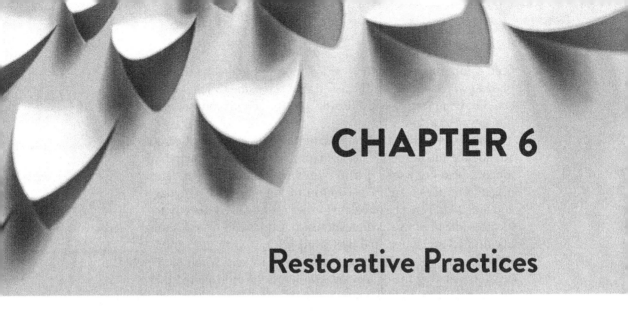

CHAPTER 6

Restorative Practices

RICARDO'S STORY

Ricardo was born and raised in Honduras. When he began first grade, his mother left the country and migrated to the United States in search of a better life and to provide economic support for Ricardo and his maternal grandmother. During this time, Ricardo's maternal grandmother became his primary caretaker. After 10 years, Ricardo's mother brought him to the United States and enrolled him in a high school at the beginning of the school year. During the first couple of months, Ricardo was actively engaged in his classes and often asked for opportunities to help his classmates or read aloud in the reading activities for the whole class. In many ways, Ricardo's quick grasp of academic content and confidence in speaking English made him a role model for other students in his class.

After a couple of months, Ricardo's attendance began to suffer, and Mr. Pérez, his English as a second language (ESL) teacher, noticed a steep decline in academic performance in his class. Mr. Pérez began to check-in with Ricardo on the days he came to school: "*¿Cómo te sientes? ¿Cómo está todo en la casa y con tu familia?* [How are you feeling? How are things back home with your family?]" Ricardo would often respond with "Everything good, Mr. Pérez. *Muchas gracias por preguntar* [Thank you for asking]," with a smile on his face.

Mr. Pérez began to notice, however, that Ricardo's eyes were sad. Mr. Pérez had a feeling that everything was not "good," so he emailed all of Ricardo's teachers to check in with them and asked about his performance in their classes. As he'd feared, Ricardo's performance was declining in all his classes, and his attendance issues were also placing him at risk of failing the quarter. Mr. Pérez had been communicating with Ricardo's mother for a while through phone conversations, but he asked that she come to school so they could have a meeting with Ricardo and the school counselor to find a way to help Ricardo.

In their meeting, the conversation revolved around Ricardo's attendance and academic performance. The counselor, who had much experience working with high school immigrant students, began to notice Ricardo's discomfort through his body language and asked Mr. Pérez to translate for her as she talked directly to Ricardo. She began to ask questions—personal questions—about his physical and emotional well-being. Ricardo, who remained silent for most of the meeting, broke down in tears when Mr. Pérez began translating the counselor's questions. Ricardo shared that he had been having issues managing his emotions and feelings at home and in school. When he was 4 years old, his father was shot and killed by a gang member in front of him while he was playing on the front porch of his house, and this traumatic memory had stayed with him, unresolved, unsupported, and unmanaged throughout his life.

In addition to dealing with the strong emotions resulting from the traumatic event of his father's murder, Ricardo shared that he did not understand where he belonged. When Ricardo came to the United States, he came to live with his mother, stepfather, and two younger, U.S.-born siblings. He had not seen his mother for over 12 years, and he was meeting his stepfather and two younger siblings for the first time. Ricardo saw himself as an outsider, as a person who did not belong in their household. All of these emotions became overwhelming for Ricardo, and he could not understand what these emotions meant, how to manage them, or how to reach out to ask for help.

Ricardo's story is a real story. Many times, formal education's obsession with academic teaching and learning does not support English learners' (ELs') social, emotional, and mental well-being. ELs and students at large are often punished by our formal education system for needing support that schools are not equipped to provide. This realization creates tension in teachers, as we witness our students' desperate need for such support inside and outside of our learning spaces. As teachers, we sometimes wonder what formal education would be like if we prioritized students' social, emotional, and mental well-being as much as we prioritize academics and standardized testing in our schools. How much better would our communities and societies be in a world where formal education prioritizes human beings' affective needs and self-awareness first or in conjunction with academic teaching? Our societies have experienced so many abrupt changes in recent years, and yet formal education has remained relatively unchanged. How are we, teachers and stakeholders concerned with the success and well-being of our students, preparing them to meet these abrupt, difficult changes with a strong heart and a positive mindset? How are we creating spaces for students and teachers to connect at a personal level, address emotional struggles, and heal? These are just some of the many questions we often ponder. In our meditations, we often circle back to the same word: *restoration*. We believe preparing our children for the future must begin with spaces welcoming the restoration of the self.

THINK BOX

According to Amstutz and Mullet (2015), discipline through a restorative lens

- recognizes the purposes of misbehavior,
- addresses the needs of those harmed,
- identifies the harm committed and finds ways to solve conflict,
- aims to improve the future,
- seeks to heal, and
- eses collaborative processes.

Think of a time when you disciplined a student. Did the approach you take to disciplining this student include the six points proposed by Amstutz and Mullet (2015)? What could you have done differently?

Jot down your responses to these questions and keep reading to learn more information about this topic. Then, return to your responses and reflect on how you can improve them.

What Is Restoration?

The word *restoration* is often defined as bringing something (or someone) back to a former position or condition. We use *restoration* as a verb to describe the reconstruction or rebuilding of something that has been altered. On the other hand, when we use the word *restoration* to describe a process occurring to human beings, we often associate it with recovery, renewal, and healing.

Restoration, as the process of making or becoming healthy again, is a vital concern for English language teachers. Our students are exposed to daily occurrences in their lives where their social, emotional, and mental well-being are affected to various degrees, and, without proper tending, these events can have long-lasting negative effects. Similarly, simple things like the words we use, the tone in which we speak, or our body language may cause unintended fragmentations and tensions in our personal and professional relationships that may also have long-lasting negative effects if they are not addressed. In restorative practices (RPs), the word *restoration* highlights the need to build healthy relationships by repairing harm between individuals and in the community.

MEET THE TEACHER

Christel Young

STEM Integrationist Teacher
Chattanooga Girls Leadership
Academy, Chattanooga,
Tennessee, USA

When I met Eliana, she was a bright-eyed high school senior. She was compliant with our school's strict policies. Even when her face wore a look of sheer exhaustion, she was at school.

During the last semester of the year, I noticed that she would fall asleep at the beginning of our class, which was a required senior capstone project class. She would fight to stay awake, but her efforts were not successful. She later confided in me that she had been having long nights and that walking around the building would help her wake up. I gave her the space to navigate her new normal and figure out what she felt was best for her.

Soon, this behavior started to show up in her other classes. She would fall asleep, and the quality of her work decreased significantly. Her school performance was placing her at risk of failing her senior classes and receiving referrals and other punishments implemented at our school. Guided by a restorative lens, I met with her and the other senior advisors to create a plan that would get her across the finish line. Eliana did her best to follow the plan, but her efforts did not satisfy the requirements for some of the courses, so a parent conference was scheduled.

At our parent conference, the interpreter revealed that Eliana was working every day until midnight (or later) to help her family's financial situation. She would then get up early in the morning and come to school. Eliana and her family were struggling financially, so quitting her job was not an option. At the same time, Eliana was so close to graduation that, even exhausted, she would come to school every day. I was opposed to the punitive methods employed in response to Eliana's situation by a school that offered her little flexibility. She was being punished by the school simply because of her family's situation—this was unfair. ➜

I was determined to help Eliana succeed, prioritize her social-emotional needs, and restore her confidence. While my course was just as important as the other classes, if she needed a rest break, I supplied space for her to rest. If she needed to go to another space to do work, I allowed her to do so—even if she needed to complete work for another course. I let her complete it, and I created an alternative plan for her to complete her senior capstone project for my class at a different time. Negotiating an assessment-driven learning environment could not eclipse the importance of Eliana's mental and physical well-being.

The brightness of Eliana's smile shone brightly from behind the mask she donned for the outdoor graduation ceremony. As she walked across the stage for graduation, I was reminded that my efforts were well worth it to see this moment. Her confidence was restored. Her future was restored. And it was well worth it. ✥

What Are Restorative Practices?

According to the International Institute for Restorative Practices, RPs are defined as "a social science that studies how to build social capital and achieve social discipline through participatory learning and decision-making" (Wachtel, 2016, p. 2). Following knowledge, paradigms, and frameworks grounded in traditional Indigenous practices from North America and around the world, RPs hope to improve communities by improving human behavior and by restoring human relationships and repairing harm (Pentón Herrera & McNair, 2021). In recent years, school settings have been incorporating RPs as a way to reimagine the commonly practiced punitive, exclusionary forms of discipline (Pentón Herrera & McNair, 2021). Many representations, names, and understandings of RPs are shared in publications today. However, for clarity, we will approach RP in this chapter and book as a philosophy and practice educators can incorporate in their pedagogy to (a) reflect inward, (b) reenvision discipline through an inclusive perspective, and (c) repair harm. Figure 6.1 shows an overview of what RP looks like in practice.

In the classroom, RPs can be incorporated in many ways and forms; educators should think of them as a continuum ranging from informal to formal practices. Figure 6.2 shares an overview of how that continuum might look in our English language classrooms. Keep in mind that the information shared in this figure and throughout the chapter can be modified to your teaching context and the English level of your students.

REFLECT INWARD	REENVISION DISCIPLINE THROUGH AN INCLUSIVE PERSPECTIVE	REPAIR HARM
Reflecting inward means paying close attention to our beliefs and how those beliefs are manifested in our behaviors. Educators following a restorative practices paradigm often engage in deep self-reflections to understand how their behavior affects them and others.	Reenvisioning discipline through an inclusive perspective is exactly what it means—offering our students with options that allow them to maintain their dignity and that help them correct their behavior, instead of punishing them for it.	When harm has been done by someone—for example, teacher to student, student to teacher, or student to student—positive steps are taken to repair the relationship and learn from this experience. In this process of repairing harm, the individual causing the harm needs to be leading the process of acknowledging and repairing the harm.
Questions to Consider • What biases are we carrying with us? These biases may be cultural, linguistic, racial, social, etc. • What are we doing to confront and demystify those biases for our benefit and the benefit of our students? • Are biases affecting the way we teach and support our students? If so, what are we doing to correct this? • Are biases influencing the way we look at behavioral problems and resolutions? If so, what are we doing to correct this?	**Questions to Consider** • What "corrective" practices is your school enforcing on students? • Do students have a voice in how they are "disciplined" or supported at school? • Are the current "corrective" practices excluding or physically removing students from the learning environment? • Are students gaining explicit knowledge of how to grow from this incident?	**Steps to Consider** • Step 1: Individuals causing the harm are given the opportunity to identify the harm caused and to whom. • Step 2: Individuals causing the harm are given the opportunity to consider and acknowledge how their behavior affected others by identifying the emotions they felt when they caused harm and the feelings they may have caused to those affected. • Step 3: Individuals causing the harm propose and implement a plan (or steps) to repair the harm caused and rebuild the relationship.

Figure 6.1 Restorative practices: From philosophy to practice.

Why Incorporate Restorative Practices in English Language Teaching?

As educators, incorporating RPs in our teaching and pedagogy gives us the knowledge to create an environment where our students can reflect on and learn how their behavior and actions affect them and those around them. RPs also equip us with techniques we can use to acknowledge when harm has been committed and implement practices to seek resolution and reparation. Lastly, RPs also give us the opportunity to reflect on our practices and decisions, and give us the opportunity to reflect on our own biases and to become more empathetic toward ourselves and our students.

Ricardo's story, shared at the beginning of this chapter, occurred at a time before Mr. Pérez knew about RPs. Back then, Mr. Pérez and his school followed what is known as a "zero-tolerance" approach to behavior management, which many times affected both the students and Mr. Pérez. When the school counselor scheduled the meeting with Ricardo's mother, the intended resolution was to suspend Ricardo for a week and not allow him to complete any pending work from any class. They believed this zero-tolerance practice of punishing Ricardo would send a strong statement that they were not going to tolerate his poor grades and attendance issues. This practice was very common in their school, but looking back, they

Informal				Formal
(Can be incorporated daily in our classes)				(Formal procedures often involve additional professional stakeholders)
AFFECTIVE STATEMENTS	AFFECTIVE DIALOGUES	RESTORATIVE INTERVENTIONS	RESTORATIVE CIRCLES	FORMAL RESTORATIVE CONFERENCES
Depending on the English level of your class, this activity may be as simple as a daily warm-up activity where students complete sentence starters, like "I am a good person because _____."	Affective dialogues give students the opportunity to engage in conversations with classmates where they recognize emotions and empathize with others.	Restorative interventions often take the form of small, impromptu meetings to address specific concerns or harm and focus on ways to repair them.	Restorative circles are one of the most distinct features of restorative practices. Conduct restorative circles as a whole-class or small groups. Educators should be trained as circle keepers before conducting restorative circles.	Formal restorative conferences involve bringing together offenders, those affected, and additional individuals who can provide support to acknowledge the harm done and agree on steps toward reparation and healing.

Figure 6.2 Continuum of restorative practices in the English language classroom.

NOTE: *Because educators should be trained as circle keepers to conduct restorative circles, we did not include activities or information about restorative circles in this chapter. For more information on how to become a restorative circle keeper, check The International Institute for Restorative Practices (IIRP)'s website (iirp.edu) and/or communicate with your school district's restorative practices coordinator.*

now understand that it was neither empathetic nor helpful for Ricardo or students like him who are carrying very heavy emotional baggage without any support.

Thankfully, Ricardo's meeting ended up on a positive note for him and his mother—the school counselor and Mr. Pérez connected both of them with a licensed mental health counselor who volunteered at a nonprofit organization in the community. Ricardo began to meet with the mental health counselor on a biweekly basis at the nonprofit organization, and his mother would accompany Ricardo on these visits from time to time. Also, with the support of the school counselor, Mr. Pérez reached out to all of Ricardo's teachers, and they worked on a plan to make up all the missing work from that quarter. Real life stories like this one happen to our students and teachers every day in our schools.

Are zero-tolerance practices beneficial for students? The response, in our experience, is a resounding *no*. Through RP, educators can create physical and virtual learning spaces that tend to our students' social, emotional, and mental well-being and that respond to harm and conflict restoratively.

MEET THE TEACHER

Robin L. McNair

*Restorative Practices Practitioner/
Coordinator*

*Prince George's County Schools,
Upper Marlboro, Maryland, USA*

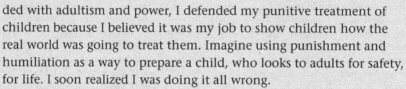

"I am preparing students for the
real world" is a frequent statement I
hear from educators during RPs training. I can recall a time in which I shared
the same sentiment. As an educator embed-
ded with adultism and power, I defended my punitive treatment of
children because I believed it was my job to show children how the
real world was going to treat them. Imagine using punishment and
humiliation as a way to prepare a child, who looks to adults for safety,
for life. I soon realized I was doing it all wrong.

Regardless of your race, nationality, or gender, we all have a universal need to feel safe. I began using RPs in my classroom as a way
to build relationships and create a sense of belonging for all of my
students. We created classroom agreements on how we wanted to be
treated by one another in order for everyone to feel safe and accepted.

ELs tend to come into a new space with feelings of isolation, and
oftentimes abandonment, having left their family members in their
home country. When I received ELs in my class, I used the circle
process of RPs to welcome them and ensure they would feel a sense
of belonging. In the circle, we would play team-building games and
music, which did not require extensive use of English, but offered
them a chance to laugh and dance with the other students. No matter
what country you are from, music brings people together.

Using RPs was also a way to honor the dignity of every student
who was part of a conflict. RPs gave everyone impacted by a conflict
the opportunity to express how they had experienced harm from that
conflict and, most important, to hear and process how others were
impacted by that same incident. ELs and non-ELs alike have a voice in
this practice. By asking five restorative questions, students get to exercise their social-emotional competencies, which is another universal
need: maintaining social-emotional agency.

Restorative Questions	SEL Competency
1. What happened? ⟷	Self-awareness
2. What were you thinking/ ⟷ feeling at the time?	Self-awareness

3. Who do you think was ←——→ Social-awareness
   impacted, and how?
4. What do you think you need ←——→ Responsible decision-making;
   to do to make things right?   relationship skills
5. What support do you need ←——→ Self-awareness; responsible
   to do that?   decision-making

When you provide spaces where diverse students can come together and have a conversation that is not blaming or shaming, children feel empowered to work toward making the internal changes they need to make better choices when conflict happens. ❖

THINK BOX

Think of a time when a comment, look, or movement created an uncomfortable or tense environment in your personal or professional life. For example, yelling at a student in front of the class or not interjecting when a student made fun of another classmate.

- What steps were taken to repair the harm caused among those involved?
- Did the steps taken to repair harm, if any, contribute to preserving a healthy relationship among those involved?
- Keeping in mind the outcome of this situation, what would you have done differently?

Jot down your responses to these questions and keep reading to learn more information about this topic.

SEL in Action

In this section, we propose three lessons you can use to introduce RPs in your English language classroom. The se lessons focus on reflecting inward (Lesson 1), on reenvisioning discipline and punishment (Lesson 2), and on exploring how to best repair harm (Lesson 3). Keep in mind that these lessons should be modified and tailored to fit your students' ages, English levels, and individual needs. Also, depending on the length of your classes, these lessons may require more than one class period to complete.

Lesson 1: Reflecting Inward

Language Objectives

Students will be able to engage all four primary language domains (listening, speaking, reading, and writing) to explore their identities and values by reflecting inward. Also, students will be able to respond to the "why" for selecting those identities and share with peers.

Content Objectives

Students will be able to reflect inward to examine their identity and values, and reasons for choosing them, and will engage in conversations with peers.

SEL Core Competencies

Self-awareness, social awareness, and relationship skills. In addition to aligning with the SEL core competencies, this lesson also aligns with Principle 1 ("know your learners"), Principle 2 ("create conditions for language learning"), Principle 3 ("design high-quality lessons for language development"), Principle 4 ("adapt lesson delivery as needed"), and Principle 5 ("monitor and assess student language development") from *The 6 Principles for Exemplary Teaching of English Learners®*.

Materials

"Reflecting Inward" worksheet (Appendix B; one per student or downloaded for student use in an online course)

Assessment

Formative or informal assessments for this lesson can be based on students' engagement in this activity and communication with their classmates. Appendix B can be collected at the end of this activity as a summative assessment, and students can also be asked to complete a Venn diagram to compare and contrast their responses with their peers'.

Procedure

RPs aim to identify the motivation of actions and shed clarity on the effect those actions have on the individual doing the action and on others. For this reason, practitioners of RPs seek to understand individuals' actions by asking *what* and *why* questions. In this activity, you and your students have the opportunity to engage in self-exploration by asking *what* and *why* questions about your identities and motivations, helping you gain a deeper understanding of yourselves, and situating yourselves as individuals in your society. In order for people to build healthy relationships with others, they must first understand who they are and how they see themselves.

Begin your class with a simple question: "Who are you?" Ask this question to one or two students. When you ask this question to students, they will probably respond with their names. After you have asked the same question to two or three students, then ask a couple of other students the question: "Who am I?" Your students will probably respond with your name. Write your name on the board as your students respond to your second question. At this point, ask them, "Am I the teacher?" Your students will respond "yes." Then add the word "teacher" below your name. Then add two to three additional words, values, or ideas of your choice that describe you. Following is an example of how your board might look:

1. Ms. Gonzáles
2. Teacher
3. Hispanic woman
4. Daughter of immigrants
5. Bilingual

When you have completed this list on the board, explain to your students why you chose these words, values, or ideas to describe and identify yourself. In this activity, the words, values, or ideas in the list describe the *what*; in other words, what words, values, or ideas describe you? Then, explain *why* they describe you, starting with each list item individually, and then all of them as a group. For example:

1. *Ms. Gonzáles* describes me because that is my father's last name that was passed down to me.
2. *Teacher* describes me because I am a teacher. I always wanted to be a teacher.
3. *Hispanic woman* describes me because my family is from Cuba.
4. *Daughter of immigrants* describes me because I am proud of my parents, who migrated to the United States from Cuba.
5. *Bilingual* describes me because I am proud to speak both English and Spanish.

These five things describe me because they tell my story, my family's story, and who I am as an individual.

After modeling this activity, check for understanding, and invite students to do the same. Provide a copy of the "Reflecting Inward" worksheet (Appendix B) to each student and invite them to include four to five words, values, or ideas of their choice that describe them. When students complete the worksheet, encourage them to share with their classmates as a whole class activity or in small groups. Depending on the time available for your class, you could also ask students to complete a Venn diagram to compare and contrast their and their peers' responses to the worksheet. By the end of this activity, you and your students will have a better understanding of everyone's identities.

Lesson 2: Reenvision Discipline and Punishment

Language Objectives
Students will be able to engage all four primary language domains (listening, speaking, reading, and writing) to evaluate how effective punishment practices are at their school and to propose appropriate consequences for actions.

Content Objectives

Students will be able to identify consequences of actions or events, evaluate their effectiveness, and argue in favor of effective consequences for students' actions and behavior.

SEL Core Competencies

Social awareness and responsible decision-making. In addition to aligning with the SEL core competencies, these lessons also align with Principle 1 ("know your learners"), Principle 2 ("create conditions for language learning"), Principle 3 ("design high-quality lessons for language development"), Principle 4 ("adapt lesson delivery as needed"), and Principle 5 ("monitor and assess student language development") from *The 6 Principles for Exemplary Teaching of English Learners®*.

Materials

Board or other surface to write student responses and reactions.

Assessment

Formative or informal assessments for this lesson can be based on students' engagement in this activity and communication with their classmates. For summative assessments, students can submit their written responses and explain the reason behind their choices.

Procedure

In traditional school systems, punishment is done *to* students when they behave or act in a way that is deemed inappropriate. As such, consequences for students' actions are selected by teachers and administrators, and these consequences are often not connected to the misbehavior. For example, in my (Luis's) high school, students would get in-school detention for not completing homework. Under a zero-tolerance paradigm such as that one, students have little, if any, voice in how they are disciplined and are deprived of the opportunity to clearly understand what harm was done and how to constructively restore an injured relationship. Through a restorative discipline lens, however, the school leadership works *with* students to select a natural consequence for the misbehavior.

To begin this activity, ask students to share common punishment practices enforced at your school. Some common forms of punishment may include suspension from school, in-school detention, not accepting late work, and, in the most severe cases, school expulsion. As you ask students about these forms of punishment, allow them to share short anecdotes or experiences related to punishment from school if they wish to do so. As students share some examples of punishment, write them down on the board and ask the reason. (What may cause students to receive this form of punishment in our school?) Some students may say, for example, that if they have come late to school for 5 consecutive days, they may receive a 3-day suspension. To help them visualize your conversation, write the information students are sharing aloud on the board or somewhere visible.

Also, make sure to clearly identify the behavior/scenario and the consequences/punishment. For example:

Student Behavior/Scenario	Consequences/Punishment
Student came to school late for 5 consecutive days	3-day suspension from school
Student was involved in a fight with other classmates	5-day suspension from school and no opportunity to turn in missed classwork

Then, ask students the following questions (and remember to modify the questions to better fit your teaching context):

- Do you think students are given the opportunity to explain *why* they acted this way?
- Do you think students learn from the types of punishment given by our school?
- In the example of coming in late to school and being suspended, do you see any connection between the action the consequence?
- In the example of being involved in a fight with other classmates, how do you think school suspension and not turning in classwork will help students understand the harm done and how to repair their relationship?

As you and your students engage in this difficult but important discussion about actions and consequences, consider dividing the class into smaller groups if your class is large. On the other hand, if you have a small number of students in your learning space, then consider arranging the classroom in an open style—a circle, for example—so everyone feels welcome to share their opinions. Through this conversation, check for understanding and ask students to keep notes on what they consider to be appropriate consequences for specific actions considered inappropriate at school and to explain the reason why. Through this activity, students have the opportunity to reenvision discipline and punishment, share their voice, and learn about actions and consequences.

Depending on your school leadership's willingness to listen to students, your ELs may share their responses and suggestions with administrators in writing or via oral presentations in your learning space. RPs ask administrators to engage in continuous self-reflection and to examine their practices (Costello et al., 2009). Listening to ELs' stories, realities, and suggestions will prove empowering for students and a critical learning experience for teachers, administrators, and school leaders.

Lesson 3: Repairing Harm

Language Objectives

Students will be able to engage all four primary language domains (listening, speaking, reading, and writing) to analyze how to repair harm.

Content Objectives

Students will be able to explore, dialogue, problem-solve, and build relationships with peers by identifying harm caused and ways to rebuild relationships with those harmed.

SEL Core Competencies

Self-awareness, social awareness, relationship skills, and responsible decision-making. In addition to aligning with the SEL core competencies, these lessons also align with Principle 1 ("know your learners"), Principle 2 ("create conditions for language learning"), Principle 3 ("design high-quality lessons for language development"), Principle 4 ("adapt lesson delivery as needed"), and Principle 5 ("monitor and assess student language development") from *The 6 Principles for Exemplary Teaching of English Learners®*.

Materials

Flashcards with specific examples of harm committed in the school or classroom.

Assessment

Formative or informal assessments for this lesson can be based on students' engagement in this activity and communication with their classmates and in their groups. For summative assessment, you may ask each group to turn in a small poster or paper with their response (one small poster or paper per group).

Procedure

A primary concern of RPs is working toward the resolution of conflict, repairing harm caused, and rebuilding relationships. To do this, schools and classrooms need to create spaces where existing conflicts are explored, explained, and acknowledged as a source causing harm to someone. Also, when harm has been identified, the individual who has caused the harm needs to be encouraged to acknowledge the harm and the effect this harm had for the person suffering, and to offer solutions to repair the harm committed. In this activity, ELs have the opportunity to explore in groups different scenarios where harm has been committed and find ways to resolve conflict and heal harm. A variation of talking about these examples could be asking students to role-play the scenarios.

To preplan for this class, create short scenarios (three to five sentences, depending on your ELs' language levels) about real examples that your school or classroom has witnessed where harm has been committed. This activity works best in small groups (four to six students). To ensure all groups have the same information, write down (or make copies of) each scenario on a flash card so every group will have the same scenarios. Also, number each scenario for all groups so students can easily identify which scenario you are discussing. For an idea of how these scenarios might look, see the following four examples from Teaching Tolerance (n.d.):

> **Scenario 1.** Jenny has taken a number of different school supplies from her classroom. She takes pencils, paper and even technology. No one is sure what she is doing with all the supplies she takes, but a number of other students as well as teachers have caught her in action. One day, her teacher comes upon her putting a school iPad into her backpack.
>
> **Scenario 2.** Lou and Django keep getting into fights at recess. Django complains that Lou bothers him because he isn't as good at sports, and Django retaliates by mocking Lou's hair and clothing. One day, the argument escalates, and the two of them end up in a physical altercation.
>
> **Scenario 3.** Meghan is having trouble in English class. Instead of seeking help, she begins acting out in class. She disrupts, calls out and laughs at other students, especially when they have the answers right. Sometimes she even sings out loud and makes other noises while the rest of the class is trying to work.
>
> **Scenario 4.** Bode shows up for school one day and decides he's had enough. He leaves the school building and hides out at a nearby park. His parents think he is at school and get very confused when his teacher calls to check up on how he is feeling.

To start the lesson, explain to students that in this class you will identify harm committed, identify how this harm may have affected those involved, and find solutions to resolve this conflict and heal the relationship(s) among those involved. Then, give each group of students the flashcards with scenarios and ask them to read together a specific scenario of your choice. Depending on your ELs' level and preference, you may wish to read the scenario aloud for the whole class while students follow your reading. Then, they can read it a second time together in their groups. After students have read this first scenario, have four to six questions prepared so students can talk about them in their groups and then present together for the whole class their interpretation and solutions. The following scenario example, which occurred in a real school, is accompanied by questions that ELs can explore together. We recommend that you create scenarios that happened at your school or in your classroom because they will be more meaningful for your ELs.

Scenario #1

Julio and Miguel are from Guatemala and are studying English in the United States. Julio speaks Spanish. Miguel is Indigenous Maya and speaks Ixil and Spanish. Miguel mispronounces a Spanish word and Julio calls him "*indio bruto* [stupid Indian]."

Questions

- In this scenario, what harm occurred?
- Who did the harm, and who is affected by this harm?
- How is this harm going to affect the relationship between Julio and Miguel?
- What type of punishment does the offender deserve for his behavior?
- What type of support and healing does the person offended need after this event?
- What can the offender do to acknowledge and heal the harm he did?

As students begin to explore each scenario and respond to the questions in groups, walk around the classroom to learn from students, observe their reactions, and check for understanding. Also, ask students to record their responses to later present in front of the class. Depending on time, you may choose to ask students how this activity made them feel and provide space in your lesson where students can share their emotions and reactions to this activity without judgement.

MEET THE TEACHER

Michelle Ivette Marrero Colón

English Learner Secondary Teacher

Arlington Public Schools, Arlington, Virginia, USA

About 2 months ago, my principal contacted me and asked, "Do you know an Edgar López? He called the school searching for you and left his number." My mind immediately went approximately 15 years back to the time when Edgar was a student at our high school. Within minutes, I called Edgar, and he shared that he had been wanting to contact me for years to express his sincere gratitude for making a significant impact in his life. He described →

how grateful he was for having an educational experience that provided him a learning environment that was welcoming, safe, stress-free, and built on a foundation of trust. Edgar also indicated that he had felt like a valued member of the classroom community where he and his classmates were willing to take risks as they supported one another. He also stated that the positive encouragement provided by me, his teacher, and daily quotes, which were part of the classroom routine, helped him to solve problems he had encountered through the many challenges in his life.

This was not the first time I had heard a student share thoughts like Edgar's. At that moment, as I internalized and reflected on my own experiences as a teacher, I was reaffirmed that RPs are a means to promote positive behaviors in classrooms incorporating an inclusive learning environment, building relationships, and resolving conflicts through problem-solving in a nonconfrontational way. I find RPs beneficial when working with adolescent ELs. Through the implementation of restorative and social-emotional practices, I have witnessed students' academic growth in language and cognitive development. Students are focused on learning and spending more time on tasks.

Meeting the social-emotional needs of adolescent ELs requires, first and foremost, building relationships and creating a stress-free learning environment where all cultures and languages are valued. For example, I greet each student by their name, with a smile, and try to say hello in their home languages. If I mispronounce a word, the student might laugh and correct me and come to realize that learning is about taking risks. Furthermore, my students and I are constantly learning from one another and teaching each other how to say hello and other words in our home languages. This social interaction creates a fun learning environment where it is acceptable to make mistakes as we all work together in building a sense of community that promotes cultural sensitivity.

Establishing high expectations is an integral part of social-emotional learning. This is accomplished by setting clear classroom routines. Classroom routines have a positive effect on anxiety levels and the affective filter. For instance, as part of the daily routine, students pick up their journals from a crate and look for the quote of the day on the SMART Board. This warm-up activity consists of a daily life quote by people from diverse backgrounds. Topics include goal setting, responsible decision-making, establishing healthy friendships and relationships, time management, self-awareness, and motivation.

First, students read the quote on their own. Then, they discuss it with members of their group (students are seated in groups of four) as international music is played in the background. During this group discussion, students speak about what they think the quote means and provide examples of how they can apply the message in their life. In addition to supporting the social-emotional needs of students ➜

in a relaxed learning environment, this activity allows students to practice all language domains as they are engaged in completing the task. Following the discussion, students write a paragraph analyzing the quote. In the paragraph, students answer questions, such as *What do you think this quote means?*, *Why is this quote significant?*, and *How can you apply it to your life?* As they write, students are utilizing higher order thinking skills, self-reflecting on past experiences, and exploring possibilities for future goals. Most important, this exercise allows students to develop competencies of social-emotional learning, which are self and social awareness, self-management, relationship skills, and effective decision-making.

At the end of the year, students reflect on their learning experience in my class. They complete a survey to provide feedback about my teaching practices and their self-reflection as students. Survey results indicate that most students identify the quote of the day activity as their favorite. According to their responses, this activity helps with creating an engaging, nonrigid classroom environment that promotes self-reflection about their behaviors, positive decision-making practices, and conflict resolution. Most important, the quotes have inspired and helped students through challenging life experiences. ❖

In Summary

This chapter provides three lessons you can use in your classroom to introduce RPs to your ELs. We also discussed the following:

1. A brief overview of restoration and RPs
2. The need for including RPs in English language teaching
3. How to reflect inward in the English language classroom (Lesson 1)
4. Opportunities for reenvisioning discipline and punishment (Lesson 2)
5. Ways to explore how to best repair harm (Lesson 3)

The activities shared throughout this chapter can be used for any grade or language proficiency level with accommodations based on student needs. Let's continue the dialogue online—there is still much more to explore. We can all learn from each other. Look for our conversation on social media using #SELforELs.

Conclusion

We hope you will be using many ideas, activities, and practical applications discussed in this book with students and yourself. We would like to end our book with a brief discussion about considerations, issues, and opportunities for social-emotional learning (SEL) in English language teaching.

Considerations

As teachers of English to speakers of other languages (TESOL) educators, it is important to keep in mind that we are not mental health professionals. In this book, we write from our stance as teachers who have successfully incorporated SEL with our students to help them explore and manage their social-emotional well-being in our classrooms. We believe that language classrooms, specifically, are in a privileged position to incorporate SEL because language, emotions, and thoughts are intertwined. At the same time, we understand that there are limits to what SEL can and should do for our students and teachers. SEL should never seek to replace professional mental health support or counseling services for students or teachers, and resources should be provided to those who need such support.

We would also like to emphasize that SEL and teacher and student well-being are a community effort. Local school systems, administrators, stakeholders, families, and educators should support SEL practices as a community. As the Collaborative for Academic, Social, and Emotional Learning reminds us, SEL "starts at home. Parents and families are critical partners in helping their children develop social and emotional know-how," and "community organizations that partner directly with schools offer students opportunities to practice SEL skills they are learning at home throughout the school day, and in their afterschool programming" (CASEL, 2021, para. 1–2). Accomplishing the goal of SEL—which is to develop and practice skills that students need to be successful, emotionally intelligent members of society—requires everyone's support.

Issues

An important issue that we need to understand when incorporating SEL into our practice is maintaining an asset-based perspective. There can be a stigma associated with social-emotional well-being and with prioritizing our—or someone else's—mental and emotional health. We'd like to encourage educators and those involved in the implementation of SEL to remove those stigmas from their practices and maintain an asset-based perspective. At heart, SEL seeks to improve how individuals treat themselves and others, keeping in mind that emotional intelligence and well-being are necessary skills people must develop to maintain respect and harmony in our communities. Another important reminder is that SEL practices are not only beneficial for students arriving from war-torn countries or for learners suffering from trauma. All students (and teachers) benefit from SEL.

Opportunities

For a long time, the fields of TESOL and second language acquisition have neglected affective considerations of language learning (Dörnyei, 2009). This statement is evidenced in the limited number of teacher education courses currently preparing pre- and in-service English language teachers on how to support the social-emotional needs of their learners and how to optimize and prioritize their teacher well-being. The neglect of affective considerations in language teaching and learning for both the teacher and the learner is a fertile area with many opportunities for further research and work. Similarly, schools (K–12, adult, and higher education) have traditionally prioritized cognitive and academic considerations in the professional development opportunities offered to their teachers. That is, the training that teachers receive in their schools often focuses on best teaching techniques and practices, with little in-depth training provided on social-emotional concerns and support for learners and the teachers themselves.

We encourage teachers and researchers in the field of TESOL to reimagine English language teaching from an SEL lens. To do this, teachers and researchers may need to detach themselves from the prevailing culture favoring method, technique, and students' academic progress (Hostetler, 2010) that currently dwells in our field and in many of our schools. We believe that students' and educators' emotions are at the heart of teaching, and SEL equips us with the skills we need to be better teachers and better learners. Without a doubt, for both teachers and learners, understanding and managing emotions poses a real challenge inside and outside of the classroom. As we know, very little teaching and learning can take place in our classrooms when emotions are not managed properly, affecting instructional time and the school experience. Keeping this in mind, we highly encourage teachers and researchers to place social-emotional education at the epicenter of English language teaching. We hope to continue the conversation on social media, using #SELforELs.

Appendixes

Appendix A: Responding to Conflict

Name: _____ Date: _____

Conflict Scenario

You and your friend Kwame take the school bus every morning to go to school. One day, some of the students in the bus were very loud and were playfully throwing paper balls inside the bus. The bus driver asked the students to stop throwing paper balls and continued driving. Some students stopped, but others continued throwing paper balls. One of the paper balls suddenly hits you.

Relationship Graphic

Taking into consideration the conflict scenario above, in what ways would you respond to this situation? Please use the graphics below to begin your brainstorming of five possible responses.

Conflict

Responses and Outcomes

Take a moment to reflect on the possible outcomes that each of the responses you have identified could create. As you reflect on the outcomes, identify which will be the best response to resolve this conflict in a peaceful manner and why.

_____

_____

_____

_____

_____

Appendix B: Reflecting Inward

Name: _____ Date: _____

Instructions: In each square, write a word, value, or idea of your choice that describes you. Then, write as many sentences as you like explaining *why* these words, values, or ideas describe you. Remember to follow the model: (word, value, or idea) describes me because _____.

References

Amstutz, L. S., & Mullet, J. H. (2015). *The little book of restorative discipline for schools: Teaching responsibility; creating caring climates.* Good Books.

Bajaj, M. (2008). Introduction. In M. Bajaj (Ed.), *Encyclopedia of peace education* (pp. 1–11). Information Age.

Barkley, R. A. (2020). *Taking charge of ADHD: The complete, authoritative guide for parents* (4th ed.). Guildford Press.

Beard, G. (2019). *Il dolce far niente: Mastering the Italian art of doing nothing.* Culture trip. https://theculturetrip.com/europe/italy/articles/la-dolce-far-niente-mastering-the-italian-art-of-doing-nothing/

Bertin, M. (2020). *Resilience and routines for families during the pandemic.* Mindful Schools. https://www.mindfulschools.org/implementation-stories/resilience-and-routines-for-families-during-the-pandemic/

Berzin, R. (2020). *A simple breathing exercise to calm your mind and body.* Mind Body Green Mindfulness. https://www.mindbodygreen.com/0-4386/A-Simple-Breathing-Exercise-to-Calm-Your-Mind-Body.html

Brackett, M. (2019). *Permission to feel: Unlocking the power of emotions to help our kids, ourselves, and our society thrive.* Celadon Books.

Cardimona, K. (2018). Differentiating mathematics instruction for secondary-level English language learners in the mainstream classroom. *TESOL Journal, 9*(1), 17–57. https://doi.org/10.1002/tesj.303

Cherry, K. (2020). *The 6 types of basic emotions and their effect on human behavior.* Verywell Mind. https://www.verywellmind.com/an-overview-of-the-types-of-emotions-4163976

Coady, M. R., Harper, C., & de Jong, E. J. (2016). Aiming for equity: Preparing mainstream teachers for inclusion or inclusive classrooms? *TESOL Quarterly, 50*(2), 340–368. https://doi.org/10.1002/tesq.223

Collaborative for Academic, Social, and Emotional Learning. (CASEL). (2013). *Social and emotional learning: Momentum!* https://casel.org/wp-content/uploads/2016/01/social-and-emotional-learning-momentum.pdf

Collaborative for Academic, Social, and Emotional Learning. (CASEL) (2020a). *Core SEL competencies.* https://casel.org/core-competencies/

Collaborative for Academic, Social, and Emotional Learning. (CASEL) (2020b). *History.* https://casel.org/history/

Collaborative for Academic, Social, and Emotional Learning. (CASEL) (2020c). *Measuring SEL: Using data to inspire practice.* https://measuringsel.casel.org/frameworks/

Collaborative for Academic, Social, and Emotional Learning. (2020d). *Self-care and re-energizing. CASEL guide to schoolwide SEL.* https://schoolguide.casel.org/focus-area-2/learn/self-care-and-re-energizing/

Collaborative for Academic, Social, and Emotional Learning. (2021). *SEL in homes & communities.* https://casel.org/homes-and-communities/

Committee for Children. (2016a). *The importance of employability skills: How and why educators should teach these skills.* https://www.cfchildren.org/wp-content/uploads/policy-advocacy/sel-employability-summary.pdf

Committee for Children. (2016b). *Why social and emotional learning and employability skills should be prioritized in education.* https://www.cfchildren.org/wp-content/uploads/policy-advocacy/sel-employability-brief.pdf

Costello, B., Watchel, J., & Watchel, T. (2009). *The restorative practices handbook for teachers, disciplinarians and administrators. Building a culture of community in schools.* International Institute for Restorative Practices.

Dörnyei, Z. (2009). *The psychology of second language acquisition.* Oxford University Press.

Eitner, J. (2018). Teaching 21st-century students in 20-century buildings with a 19th-century educational design [Online Presentation]. https://www.haikudeck.com/21-20-19-teaching-21st-century-students-in-a-20th-century-buildings-with-a-19th-century-educational-design-education-presentation-f71d626a83#slide0

Gaiam. (2020). *Meditation 101: Techniques, benefits, and a beginner's how-to.* https://www.gaiam.com/blogs/discover/meditation-101-techniques-benefits-and-a-beginner-s-how-to

Gee, J. P. (1989). Orality and literacy: From the savage mind to ways with words. *Journal of Education, 171*(1), 39–60. https://doi.org/10.1177/002205748917100104

Goleman, D. (2005). *Emotional intelligence: Why it can matter more than IQ.* Bantam Books.

Gotter, A. (2019). *8 breathing exercises to try when you feel anxious.* Healthline. https://www.healthline.com/health/breathing-exercises-for-anxiety

Harris, I. M., & Morrison, M. L. (2013). *Peace education* (3rd ed.). McFarland & Company.

Harvard Business Review (Ed). (2015). *On emotional intelligence.* Harvard Business Review Press.

Hastings, C., & Jacob, L. (Eds.). (2016). *Social justice in English language teaching.* TESOL International Association.

Hostetler, K. (2010). (Mis)understanding human beings: Theory, value and progress in education research. *Educational Studies, 46*(4), 400–415. https://doi.org/10.1080/00131946.2010.496351

International Society for Technology in Education. (2017). *ISTE standards for educators*. https://www.iste.org/standards/for-educators

Jara, B. (2020). *Working remote: COVID 10 principles*. Office of Inclusion and Institutional Equity.

Ladson-Billings, G. (1995). Toward a theory of culturally relevant pedagogy. *American Educational Research Journal, 32*(3), 465–491. https://doi.org/10.3102/00028312032003465

Ladson-Billings, G. (2009). *The dream-keepers: Successful teachers of African American children*. Jossey-Bass.

Linville, H. (2016). ESOL teachers as advocates: An important role? *TESOL Journal, 7*(1), 98–131. https://doi.org/10.1002/tesj.193

Mayo Clinic Staff. (2020). *Mindfulness exercises: See how mindfulness helps you live in the moment*. https://www.mayoclinic.org/healthy-lifestyle /consumer-health/in-depth/mindfulness-exercises/art-20046356

Milner, H. R., IV, Cunningham, H. B., Delale-O'Connor, L., & Kesternberg, E. G. (2019). *"These kids are out of control": Why we must reimagine "classroom management" for equity*. Corwin.

Mindworks Team. (2021). How does meditation improve memory and focus? *Mindworks*. https://mindworks.org/blog/focus-meditation/

Moore, A. R. (2016). Inclusion and exclusion: A case study of an English class for LGBT learners. *TESOL Quarterly, 50*(1), 86–108. https://doi.org/10.1002/tesq.208

Niemiec, R. M. (2017). 3 definitions of mindfulness that might surprise you: Getting at the heart of what mindfulness is. *Psychology Today*. https://www.psychologytoday.com/us/blog/what-matters-most /201711/3-definitions-mindfulness-might-surprise-you

OfficeNinjas. (2020). *How to make saying no through email easy with 9 different templates*. https://officeninjas.com/need-say-no-nicely-weve -got-9-email-templates/

Osher, D., Kidron, Y., Brackett, M., Dymnicki, A., Jones, S., & Weissberg, R. P. (2016). Advancing the science and practice of social and emotional learning. *Review of Research in Education, 40*(1), 644–681. https://doi.org/10.3102/0091732x16673595

Oxford, R. L. (2013). *The language of peace: Communicating to create harmony*. Information Age.

Oxford, R. L., Gregersen, T., Harrison, M., & Olivero, M. M. (2021). The call for peace in language education: This book's purpose, themes, and peace approach. In R. L. Oxford, M. M. Olivero, M. Harrison, & T. Gregersen (Eds.), *Peacebuilding in language education: Innovations in theory and practice* (pp. 54–92). Multilingual Matters.

Paris, D. (2012). Culturally sustaining pedagogy: A needed change in stance, terminology, and practice. *Educational Researcher, 41*(3), 93–97. https://doi.org/10.3102/0013189X12441244

Pentón Herrera, L. J. (2018). *Indigenous students from Latin America in the United States.* Informes Del Observatorio/Observatorio Reports. Cervantes Institute at the Faculty of Arts and Sciences of Harvard University. https://doi.org/10.15427/or042-08/2018en

Pentón Herrera, L. J. (2019). How to behave and why: Exploring moral values and behavior in the ESOL newcomer classroom. *TESOL Quarterly, 53*(4), 1033–1059. https://doi.org/10.1002/tesq.532

Pentón Herrera, L. J. (2020). Social-emotional learning in TESOL: What, why, and how. *Journal of English Learner Education, 10*(1), 1–16.

Pentón Herrera, L. J. (2021). Caring as a form of advocacy for literacy -emergent newcomers with special education needs: The community -building pedagogical approach in the U.S. In P. Vinogradova & J. K. Shin (Eds.), *Contemporary foundations for teaching English as an additional language: Pedagogical approaches and classroom applications* (pp. 265–269). Routledge.

Pentón Herrera, L. J., & McNair, R. L. (2021). Restorative and community -building practices as social justice for English learners. *TESOL Journal, 12*(1), 1–11. https://doi.org/10.1002/tesj.523

Puddicombe, A. (2017). What's the right amount of time to meditate? *Headspace.* https://www.headspace.com/blog/2017/05/29/right-amount -meditation/

Schlund, J., Jagers, R. J., & Schlinger, M. (2020, August). *Emerging insights: Advancing social and emotional learning as a lever for equity and excellence.* CASEL. https://casel.org/wp-content/uploads/2020/08/CASEL-Equity -Insights-Report.pdf

Screencast-O-Matic. (2019). *Video creation for everyone.* https://screencast-o-matic.com

Short, D. J., Becker, H., Cloud, N., Hellman, A. B., & Levine, L. N. (2018). *The 6 principles for exemplary teaching of English learners: Grades K–12.* TESOL International Association.

Smore. (2020). *Make a gorgeous newsletter in minutes: It is that easy.* https://www.smore.com

Srinivasan, M. (2019). *SEL every day: Integrating social and emotional learning with instruction in secondary classrooms.* W. W. Norton & Company.

Staehr Fenner, D. (2014). *Advocating for English learners: A guide for educators.* Corwin; TESOL International Association.

Strauss, R. (2017). Seven mindfulness attitudes = Your real core power. *Mindful Psychotherapy + Mindful Change.* https://www.thrivepsychothe rapyllc.com/blog/2017/11/20/seven-mindfulness-attitudes-your-real -core-power

Tantillo Philibert, C. (2018). *Everyday SEL in high school: Integrating social-emotional learning and mindfulness into your classroom.* Routledge.

Taylor, J., & Read, L. (2020). *SEL assessment must be strengths-based, but what does that mean?* CASEL. https://casel.org/sel-assessment-must-be -strengths-based-but-what-does-that-mean/

Teaching Tolerance. (n.d.). *Toolkit. Restorative justice role-playing scenarios.* https://www.learningforjustice.org/sites/default/files/2017-08/teaching -tolerance-restorative-justice-role-playing-scenarios.pdf

TESOL International Association. (2017). *English learners and ESSA: What educators need to know. A TESOL resource kit.* https://www.tesol.org/docs /default-source/ppt/tesol-essa-resource-kit-final66978542f2fd6d058c 49ff00004ecf9b.pdf?sfvrsn=0

TESOL International Association. (2021). *The 6 principles for exemplary teaching of English learners.* https://www.tesol.org/the-6-principles /the-6-principles

Room Rater [@ratemyskyperoom]. (n.d.). Tweets [Twitter profile]. Retrieved May 20, 2021, from https://twitter.com/ratemyskyperoom?lang=en

UNESCO. (2005). *Peace education: Framework for teacher education.* https://www.gcedclearinghouse.org/sites/default/files/resources /Peace%20Education.pdf

United Farm Workers. (n.d.). Education of the heart. Cesar Chavez in his own words. https://ufw.org/research/history/education-heart-cesar -chavez-words/

Urrieta, L., Jr. (2019). Indigenous reflections on identity, trauma, and healing: Navigating belonging and power. *Genealogy, 3*(2), 1–14. https://doi.org/10.3390/genealogy3020026

Wachtel, T. (2016). *Defining restorative.* International Institute for Restorative Practices. https://www.iirp.edu/images/pdf/Defining -Restorative_Nov-2016.pdf

Wenden, A. L. (1995). Critical language education. In C. Schäffner & A. L. Wenden (Eds.), *Language and peace* (pp. 211–227). Harwood Academic.

Winn, M. T., Graham, H., & Alfred, R. R. (2019). *Restorative justice in the English language arts classroom.* National Council of Teachers of English.